GET S
STAY S
NATURALLY

GET SLIM
STAY SLIM
NATURALLY

DR FRANCESCA SWAINSTON

I dedicate this book to the man of my dreams, Louis Greeff, and our long-awaited miracle daughter, Ndyana.

First published in 1997 by
Struik Publishers (Pty) Ltd
(a member of the Struik Publishing Group (Pty) Ltd)

Cornelis Struik House
80 McKenzie Street
Cape Town 8001
South Africa

Reg. No. 54/00965/07

ISBN 1 86872 117 5

Project Manager: Linda de Villiers
Cover Design: Petal Palmer
Editor: Claudia Dos Santos
Design and DTP: Claudia Dos Santos

Typesetting by Struik DTP
Reproduction by cmyk prepress, Cape Town, South Africa
Printed and bound by National Book Printers, Drukkery Street,
Goodwood, Western Cape, South Africa

PLEASE NOTE: This publication is not intended for the treatment
of any serious health disorders. While every effort has been made
to verify the facts and present clear and accurate instructions for
using the herbs, the author and publishers can accept no liability
for any injury, illness or damage which may inadvertently be
caused to the user while following these instructions.

CONTENTS

A NEW BEGINNING

M ost of us women have been on the weight-loss roller coaster since our teens. The dream of having a perfect figure was always a fantasy just out of reach. Experts and well-meaning friends tell us that the solution to our weight problem is simple – just consume less fat and fewer calories and increase your exercise. Those of us who have been fighting the battle of the bulge for years, however, know that it is not that simple. Yes, perhaps a drastic reduction of our fat or calorie intake does initially take pounds off, but inevitably, once we start eating normally again we put that weight back on, and then some! The reason this happens is because we did not rectify the cause of our weight gain.

In other words, if we were emotionally satisfied and our bodies healthy, with all the organs functioning properly, we would not be overweight. Over-eating does not cause excess fat tissue. The desire to eat more than we need is a symptom. It is the body's way of telling you that something is wrong. Yet, what do we do? We ignore the message, thinking that we simply get these uncontrollable urges to eat for some strange reason. We keep ourselves under strict control because we think we are shameless gluttons. Rest assured this is not the case. There is a deeper reason for these cravings, which is what this book will be telling you about.

A NEW BEGINNING

Few weight-loss programmes or preparations on the market today address the cause of excess fat. This is why there is a continual search for the ultimate solution – one that will work permanently and safely. This book reveals why we put on weight and provides you with an easy solution that works. Once you know the facts you can make an educated decision about how to solve your weight problem permanently. It is possible, many people have done it.

Herbs are gifts from God. Hippocrates, the father of medicine, said: 'Let your food be your medicine and your medicine be your food.' Herbs can safely cure most illnesses and are also the most effective aids in losing weight. This book is a simple guide to using herbs as a means to permanent, healthy slimness. The recipe described in the chapter entitled Creating The Formula has been in use for over six years with excellent results. So start today and transform yourself into a slim, healthy and vibrant human being.

ABOUT HERBS

*"I was warned by the hospital to lose weight. Using Natruslim I went
from 97 kg (214 lb) to 85 kg (187 lb), and that's without dieting."*
Mr C. Harris, Lansdowne

The swing to herbal medicine

Plants, including herbs, vegetables and fruit, are an effective and safe means of
regulating and healing the body. When the body and all its organs and systems are
working properly, the result is a normalisation of weight. Before herbal remedies
regained popularity during the late 80s, conventional doctors believed natural
medicine to be quackery, or based on the placebo effect where patients' symptoms
improve solely as a result of their belief in the therapy rather than due to any
actual physiological effect of the plants used. That is, improvement in the patient's
condition was thought to be entirely psychosomatic. As people became more and
more disillusioned with modern medicine and turned to natural traditional cures,
researchers conducted experiments to determine whether there were, in fact, any
therapeutic benefits to be found in natural healing methods. Intensive research
revealed proof to validate these therapies, although scientists cannot always
explain why particular herbs have healing properties, and hence the swing to
natural medicine gained momentum.

The beauty of herbs is that the active ingredient in the plant occurs together with
a myriad other substances that complement its absorption and function within the
body. Conventional drugs, however, are made by extracting the active ingredient
from a plant and administering it in large doses, based on the theory that more is
better. The manufacturing process involves removing and discarding the comple-
mentary substances which would naturally prevent the active ingredient from
becoming toxic.

This is why medicaments produced by the pharmaceutical industry often have
side effects – the body cannot deal with the active ingredients in such large doses.
Since all drugs are potentially harmful, pharmaceutical companies apply strict

controls in their manufacture. Herbal medicines, on the other hand, do not require the same stringent control because their side effects are minimal. Herbs are, in fact, food and should be as freely available. It is a basic human right to be able to obtain healing and nutritious plants. In many cultures patients consult herbalists and are given herbal mixtures. Medicines are prepared in home kitchens, often using ingredients that are also used to flavour meals. Herbal medicine and foods are so closely linked that the two cannot be separated. Haven't we all made hot toddies to ward off a developing cold?

Recently the pharmaceutical industry has done a complete about-face: the substances they previously claimed had absolutely no medicinal merit may in future become subject to stringent control. Large pharmaceutical concerns now realise that they stand to lose billions of rand if they don't gain control of the infant herbal industry, because natural medicine is becoming more popular than the harsh drug therapy popular with many conventional doctors today.

Regulating, controlling and restricting herbal medicine, as is the trend today, is bad news for the man in the street. A person can quite safely and cheaply control most cases of high blood pressure (hypertension) with a simple herbal formula that would cost around R40 a month. However, if herbs were to be subjected to the rigid controls imposed by the pharmaceutical industry, what would have cost R40 could increase to as much as R100 a month and you would need a prescription from your doctor in order to obtain it. Fortunately, in South Africa we have a strong contingency of traditional healers who have refused to allow traditional medicine to be restricted, but the battle for control still rages on as I write this book.

Herbs, unlike drugs, are a means to an end. They are used for relatively short periods to regulate and tone the organs and restore proper function to the whole body. This means that they allow the body to heal itself until, in the long run, it does not need to rely on medical intervention, be it herbs, vitamin supplements or drugs, in order to maintain health and a slim figure.

Maintaining a slim figure with ease

Once the herbal formula for slimmers has restored physiological balance in the body, resulting in achievement of your ideal weight and vibrant health, all that is necessary to maintain your figure and health is a diet that includes fresh, nutrient-rich foods. Chapters nine and ten describe a healthy eating programme and 'wonderfoods' that must be incorporated into your eating plan. Once your body is supplied with a varied, nutritious diet, there should be no need to resort to added assistance in order to lose weight and maintain your health. A balanced metabolism results in ideal weight which can be maintained at minimal cost. The only expense will be your weekly grocery bill – you no longer need to spend large amounts of money on medication, food supplements, gym registration fees and all the other gimmicks you've spent fortunes on in the past! All you need to do is choose food wisely. Wise choice and the skilled preparation of food result in a beautiful figure as well as a rebirth of the pleasure of eating.

It is important to remember that our bodies have the capacity to heal themselves, although the media and the pharmaceutical companies (including manufacturers of vitamins and food supplements) would like us to believe otherwise.

Keeping your slim figure on a low budget

All you need to maintain glowing health and a slim figure is a knowledge of what to eat and good shopping skills. Spend your money on quality foods and you will save on bills from the doctor, pharmacy and health shop.

It will be necessary to train yourself to undo years of propaganda. We have been taught that pills are necessary to cure illnesses. As soon as we feel unwell we rush off to the doctor for a prescription, or at the very least, visit the pharmacy for an over-the-counter drug to stop the symptoms from developing. Wrong action! If we took time to rest a little, and fed ourselves with nutrient-rich foods, our bodies would heal themselves – sometimes even faster than the pills could have done. However, when starting your programme, especially if you suffer from poor health, vitamin and mineral supplements and a restricted therapeutic diet may initially be useful. Many symptoms, including excess fatty tissue, occur due to a lack of one or more vitamins, which results in a poor metabolism and dysfunction of the organs. Often vitamins cannot be absorbed from food or tablets because they are too toxic, and are simply excreted in the urine. Herbs detoxify the body so that any vitamins entering the system can be fully absorbed and utilised.

I do not recommend dieting in this book – so much has already been written on the subject and by now the weight-conscious person should know how they should be eating. But Dr Paavo Airola raises a very important point in *Every Woman's Book* when she says that there are two kinds of dieting: therapeutic and preventive.

Therapeutic diets include all the radical eating and fasting regimes that have been propounded in the past, like the grape and the fat free diet, juice fasting and water fasting. These do not provide all the nutrients necessary for normal health and weight maintenance, but can be excellent tools to cure disease and restore health and ideal weight. However, once the body has been restored to its ideal weight and health it is essential to revert to a normal eating plan that comprises food from all the food groups, otherwise you'll eventually develop a deficiency in some essential nutrient and become overweight or ill again. This maintaining eating plan, which provides optimal nutrition, Dr Airola calls preventive diet.

Vitamin and mineral supplements can never replace the quality nutrients supplied by a diet of fresh, wholesome food. New healing compounds are found in foodstuffs yearly. No matter how much research is done, it will take years to discover all the healing properties in the things we eat. We cannot risk eating man-made processed foods and supplements limited by researchers' knowledge. No matter how technologically advanced the human race has become, we are still infants when it comes to understanding health, nutrition and weight management.

If we had all the answers, the world wouldn't be so full of sickly and overweight people. Ailments are becoming increasingly chronic and insidious, our immune systems are weakening and scientists have not solved the problem.

When the family was nursed back to health in grandma's time, their health was truly restored. Livelihoods and families were dependent on having fully functional members. They couldn't afford to lose the enthusiasm, drive and vitality which are often depleted by conventional drug therapy. Most of the elderly had full use of their faculties until their time came to move on; chronic depression and fatigue were unheard of; there were no institutions that looked after the unproductive members of society. This forced people to come up with healing solutions that really worked – if they hadn't, our race would probably not have been as successful as it is today.

Sadly, the global state of wellbeing is deteriorating rapidly with the advent of the idea that health comes packaged in pill-form. We have disempowered ourselves. Affluent societies have become frightened of exposure to germs due to media coverage and clever pharmaceutical marketing. We have lost the sense of security that comes from knowing our bodies are intrinsically strong and capable of healing themselves, and medicate ourselves aggressively at the first sign of infection.

Americans spend trillions of dollars on health care and South Africans are fast following in their footsteps. Continuous medication results in mass constitutional weakness. The immune system, like any other body system, strengthens from practice. If it is denied the chance to combat invading germs it will dwindle away like unused muscle tissue.

South Africans, unfortunately, are losing their rich cultural heritage of folk remedies. (One of the reasons the Boers triumphed over the English in the Anglo Boer War was that they could treat themselves with indigenous herbs, while English soldiers died from infectious diseases for which they had no treatment.) Today, even tribal medicine is being belittled, as black people strive to become westernised. All traditional lore is valuable – herbal medicine is relatively cheap and it is also extremely effective.

Not only have we been poisoned by slimming drugs and abused by knife-happy surgeons (who would have believed that doctors, who according to the Hippocratic oath are supposed to heal with the least intervention possible, could come up with the ridiculous solution of wiring fat people's jaws to prevent them from eating?), we also spend fortunes in slimming clubs and gyms. You too have probably suffered from misleading advertising as pharmaceutical companies try to milk money out of you. Yet, your weight problem can easily and cheaply be solved if you follow the guidelines in this book.

The solution for permanent weight loss is to live a healthy, fulfilling life and eat a diet rich in fresh, unadulterated foods. Take time to learn about proper eating habits and experiment with various foods and different preparation techniques. In the long run you will gain strong immunity as well as a slim figure and a positive outlook on life. This is the most important lesson we need to learn. Without good health our lives become miserable. We become powerless and dependent on institutions that often have our purses rather than our wellbeing at heart.

HERBS AS MEDICINE

*"I lost approximately 10 kg (22 lb) on two bottles of Natruslim. I used
to suffer terribly from abdominal gas and bloatedness due to having
an irritable bowel. These symptoms have completely disappeared.
My wife is ecstatic that I have lost my 'love handles'. She has also
used Natruslim which has solved her water retention problem. "*
Mr Pieter Zaayman, Mossel Bay

The whole world already uses herbs as medicinal aids

Herbs are very easy to use and you will be pleasantly surprised at just how
effective they are. In fact, you have already used herbal medicine without knowing it: drinking coffee or tea in the morning to get you going is a common example.
One of the medicinal effects of coffee is that it enhances the conscious mind, in
other words, it helps a person to think better. (It is said that coffee was originally
introduced to England as a medicine to counter the effects of drunkenness.) The
herbs used for slimming are not as common as tea, coffee and garlic, although some
cultures commonly use them as dietary ingredients.

Most nations cook with herbs and a skilled cook can combine the medicinal
agents of herbs and spices in such a way that they are delicious to eat. It is commonly known that garlic kills bacteria and lowers blood pressure. This accounts
for the lower occurrence of related afflictions in countries whose recipes call for
substantial amounts of this pungent plant. Indian cuisine is prevalently hot and
spicy which has a boosting effect on the metabolism and, as a whole, Indians are
not an obese nation. Americans, on the other hand, who frequently eat denatured,
overprocessed foods with much added sugar, salt and chemical additives, have
enormous weight problems.

What form of herb should you use

The most effective way to use herbs is in tincture form, which is much like tea,
except that alcohol, instead of water, is used as solvent . Tinctures are more effective

than tea because alcohol is capable of absorbing more from the plant than water, thereby facilitating ready absorption and utilisation of the medicinal agents. Herbs can easily be mixed to any ratio required, which is impossible with tablets. If you prefer a non-alcoholic remedy, just place the drops of tincture in a little boiling water for a few minutes until the alcohol has evaporated, leaving the active essence of the herb. This is also a good way to give the herbs to little children, although a 15-drop dose of tincture is such a small amount that it is unlikely to have any negative effect.

Tinctures are preferable to tablets because the latter contain binding agents and various additives that prevent the tablet from crumbling. In addition, the manufacture of tablets involves a lot of processing which reduces the potency of the herb in the finished product.

The quality of tinctures can vary greatly, depending on the quality and freshness of the plant material, the percentage of alcohol and the time the herb was left to steep. Most tinctures should be a rich browny reddish liquid with tiny particles dissolved in it, giving it a certain viscosity. If the tincture is a clear brown-green it may mean that it has been steeped for only a short time or has been filtered. Filtration removes healing substances from the tincture, while leaving the tincture to steep for too short a period means that many of the active ingredients remain in the plant matter and can't dissolve into the alcohol.

Price difference is usually an indication of quality. The better the quality the more effective your formula. Shop around for tinctures or make your own (see Creating the Formula, page 38) to be sure of their efficacy.

How to take herbs

Herbs should be taken on an empty stomach to ensure that they are totally absorbed and not lost in the food due to faulty digestion. However, if you forget to take the herbal drops before your meal, do take them afterwards, because it is important to take them regularly, three times a day. That isn't to say that you have to eat after taking the herbal drops as you often have to when you are on a course of conventional medicine. Herbs do not damage the lining of the digestive tract. The reason for taking them before each meal is so that you remember to take them regularly. Easiest would be to take the drops about 10 minutes before meals, which would also encourage you to eat regularly!

The usual dosage is 15–20 drops in a little glass of water, three times a day. Take 20 drops if you have a strong constitution, or if you would like to speed up your weight-loss progress. If you have a serious health condition like cancer, diabetes or cardiovascular disease, begin with 5 drops, three times daily. If no unusual symptoms develop after one week, increase the dosage to 10 drops three times a day for a week, and then increase to the normal dosage of 15 drops, three times a day. If you do experience any symptoms after increasing the dosage, don't cut down the number of drops unless you feel very uncomfortable. If the symptoms persist, cut down to the previous dosage for another week, after which try increasing again. If you are in a reasonable state of health begin with 15 drops, three times daily. If you experience symptoms like headaches and bowel or urinary changes continue the 15-drop dosage. What you are experiencing is a good indication that your body is detoxifying and healing. Any detoxification and regulatory symptoms normally disappear within 10 days. Children above the age of seven can safely take 15 drops, children from four to seven years of age should take five drops three times a day.

I must stress the importance of taking the herbs regularly. You will not see results if you take them sporadically as it takes a regular supply of the healing substances to help your body repair itself. Often, damage you are unaware of has resulted in your excess weight. Organs like the liver and thyroid (the endocrine gland controlling the metabolism) may be functioning poorly, yet you are in relatively good health and think the occasional headache or pain is just part of life. As these symptoms increase in frequency you ignore them, or take a tablet. You don't feel sick enough to consult a doctor, and, if you do, he will tell you there is nothing really wrong and prescribe some painkillers. What has happened, however, is that your system is suffering, and you are making matters worse by taking medication. This puts even more strain on your flagging organs and could also be the cause of your weight gain.

Even if you are not excessively overweight, interference in the normal body functions is bound to have produced deposits of excess fat. The balance needs to be restored in order to burn away excess fat and lose retained water. Any symptoms, including fat deposits, could be the result of years of abuse and the damage must be repaired before the problem clears up. Take the herbs regularly so that your body has continual assistance.

Holistic weight loss – the permanent solution

Using the holistic method, symptoms can only improve when the whole body begins to function properly. Rectify the underlying cause of a symptom or disease and the condition will improve.

Take, for instance, a headache which may be triggered by eating rich foods. The doctor will probably tell his patient to steer well away from rich food and prescribe a painkiller. However, fatty foods are not the cause of the headache, only the aggravating factor. The underlying cause of the headache, in this case probably a congested liver, has not been treated. The headache is simply the body's early warning signal that there is a problem requiring treatment. If the underlying cause of the headache is not cured a more serious disease will develop later. The headache is like the little red light on a car's dashboard warning the driver that fuel is running low. If the driver does not take heed and fill up, the car will, sooner or later, stop moving. No-one in their right mind would reason that the dashboard is faulty and disconnect the light. The driver fills up with petrol, thankful that he was warned in advance. Well, exactly the same model applies to your body. The headache is a signal indicating that something in the body needs to be fixed. In this case, taking herbs to decongest and regulate the liver will cure the problem with the result that the warning light, your headache, stops flashing.

The same theory applies to excess fat tissue and a ravenous appetite. Both are signs of some disorder within the body. Taking appetite suppressants or medication that alters the natural rhythm of the body is dangerous – you are not listening to your body and fixing the cause. If you don't rectify the underlying cause, you will become ill as you get older. This is why the Western world is suffering an epidemic of chronic diseases like circulatory disorders, cancer, arthritis, and others. Symptoms play an important function as early warning systems and as such must be heeded not suppressed.

Herbs are the most useful aids in combating excessive weight, water retention and cellulite because they cure the cause by helping to regulate the metabolism and all the body systems, eventually resulting in permanent weight loss. Furthermore, by using the herbal formula permanently, you will maintain the healthy weight you have achieved. If, however, you are under a lot of stress, eat a diet of overprocessed and junk food, take medication, or are experiencing major life changes such as divorce, pregnancy, job change, etc. (all of which throw the

17

body out of balance), you may possibly gain weight. If this happens, using the herbs for a short period will restore balance and normalise your weight. Be sure to start the drops as soon as you notice your weight picking up.

Should you get sick or start feeling under the weather, taking the appropriate herbs for a few days will supply vital healing substances to aid the body in restoring its health. If you do this in time, you will prevent alterations in your metabolism which, if unattended, may cause sudden weight gain. Remember: prevention is better than cure.

More and more people are choosing natural remedies, because they have become disillusioned with the empty promises of conventional medicine. Drugs prescribed by doctors often do more harm than good. A study conducted by the New England Journal of Medicine in 1994 showed that Americans made 425 million visits to holistic practitioners, compared with 338 million trips to regular doctors. This statistic is forcing the allopathic fraternity to grudgingly admit that herbs and nutrition are an important, if not crucial, factor in curative and preventive medicine. Without the increasing pressure from the public and the media, regular doctors would still be denouncing holistic medicine as quackery.

In 1991 I began a small business, selling a herbal slimming aid called Natruslim®, as well as other herbal products that I had formulated. In five years it grew from a home-based mail order business to an international company, supplying pharmacies and health shops, as well as the general public. Some of the people who lost weight using the formula couldn't believe their results. Many had tried almost everything on the market to no avail.

You will find the Natruslim® formula in Chapter 7, followed by recipes that include additional herbs for specific conditions not addressed by the basic for mula. Using herbs is a bit like concocting a potion, believe it or not! Try different combinations until you come up with the formula that works best for you. There is no reason to be cautious – these herbs have no side effects. They are completely safe for everyone, no matter what your state of health may be.

THE PROCESS OF WEIGHT LOSS

"I found my eating patterns changed when I acquired live-in help and delicious meals were prepared for me. I took one and a half bottles of Natruslim and lost 7 kg (15.5 lb), reaching my goal weight of 63 kg (139 lb). I am thrilled because once I lost 9 kg (20 lb) on a diet and regained it as soon as I came off the diet, which hasn't happened after stopping the Natruslim. The headaches which used to plague me decreased dramatically. It helped with my constipation too. My daughter gained weight after a time of depression. She went from 78 kg (172 lb) to 61 kg (134.5 lb) from two and a half months on Natruslim. Neither my daughter nor I have regained the weight and I thoroughly recommend Natruslim."
Mrs Rena Angel, Bothaville

How quickly will you lose weight?

Since we all lose weight at different rates, it is impossible to predict how much you will lose and in what period of time. Progress depends on many factors, such as general health, toxicity level in the cells, current courses of medication (including the contraceptive pill), and lifestyle. Some may lose as much as 3.6 kg (8 lb) a week, others may gain weight during the first week of the programme.

Generally speaking, obese people and individuals who retain a lot of water will lose weight fairly quickly. Those with toxins stored in their fat tissue may put on weight initially and so, although the fat is being broken down, the weight displayed on the scale will rise. This is due to a protective mechanism in the body. When fat breaks down toxins are released into the bloodstream. To prevent high concentrations of these toxins the body retains water, resulting in a gain of weight. Taking diuretic drugs at this point is dangerous as it forces the kidneys to excrete water, resulting in dangerously high levels of toxins, which may lead to illness. Nausea, dizziness, headaches and a general feeling of being unwell may occur. So do not take diuretics, continue with the herbs and drink plenty of water to help flush the toxins out of your system.

Detoxification

You may experience slight symptoms of detoxification in the first few days on the herbal programme as the fat tissue starts breaking down, even if you start losing weight immediately. Remember that it has taken your body years to reach its present levels of toxicity and that therefore the eliminatory process may take some time. How quickly your body is restored to a more natural harmony depends on how toxic your system is, as well as the state of your eliminatory organs such as the kidneys and liver, and your basic metabolic rate. Symptoms of detoxification include bloating, headaches, body aches, tiredness, changes in mood, bowel and urinary changes and discharges, including colds. Again, continue taking the drops and drink plenty of water. Detoxification is essential for permanent weight loss to occur.

It is important not to take any medication that interferes with the detoxification process, otherwise the procedure is prolonged and weight loss will be postponed until the body can resume eliminating toxins unhindered once again. If you do experience any of the aforementioned symptoms, rest assured that your body is beginning to cleanse and heal itself, and give it all the assistance and support it needs. This can include drinking lots of water, resting, eating a frugal diet of raw, fresh fruits and vegetables for a few days, or even a juice fast. (See Recommended Reading for sources of further information.) Sometimes it is necessary to feel a little discomfort in order to gain health, and we should not be afraid of it – the symptoms will pass within a few days. Our bodies are stronger than we give them credit for.

If you don't use your muscles they will waste away. Well, the same applies to your immune system. Our immune systems have begun to waste away over the years because of disuse, giving rise to the chronic auto-immune diseases prevalent today. Popping tablets every time we get a cold or feel slightly ill is no solution – so be brave and trust in your body.

Before we had all the over-the-counter preparations available today, our constitutions were strong because they fought invading germs with fever. Nowadays fever is suppressed and offending micro-organisms killed off with antibiotics. In future we may become entirely dependent on drugs as our bodies lose the ability to protect themselves altogether. Do not make the mistake of thinking that the programme doesn't work. Persevere, and within days you'll begin losing weight and will feel energetic, vibrant and healthy.

You really need to change your perspective: herbs do not take over the protective function but strengthen the body by assisting it in fighting its own battles against invading micro-organisms. If you experience any detoxification symptoms, don't panic. However, if there is no improvement after a few days, you may want to seek medical advice. Please remember that only a very small percentage of people that have used the formula reported any symptoms, so don't be afraid. Detoxification is a crucial part of permanent weight loss, and you will feel so much better after your body has successfully eliminated the toxins that it accumulated over the years.

Weight loss does not mean fat loss

Do not use a scale to record your weight-loss progress. Weight is not a true indication of the amount of fat in the body. There is a general misunderstanding about fat and weight. Being heavy doesn't mean you're fat. Similarly, you may not be overweight and yet it is possible that you have excess fat tissue. Weight experts now talk about a fat-muscle ratio which is a much truer indicator of whether a person carries too much fat.

Muscle tissue weighs a lot more than the same volume of fat tissue. If you were to go on a strict, calorie-controlled diet it would be possible to become thinner, and if you are an old hand at dieting you've probably gone this route already, as it is the most common method used in the attempt to lose excess fat. What happens, though, is that you lose both muscle and fat tissue, as well as water and bone mass.

The reason why you don't only lose fat tissue is that you are depriving your body of vital nutrients. Even choosing a well-balanced eating plan that includes all the essential vitamins and minerals does not necessarily prevent a nutrient deficiency. We need a healthy digestive system and metabolism to break down, absorb and use the nutrients efficiently. If the function of any organ or system is disordered, the result is a deficiency in one or more nutrients. This can happen even if you are eating properly. The resultant lack of nutrients causes an increase in appetite and unusual cravings, which are the loyal companions of most dieters.

Many people put on more weight than they lose on the yo-yo diet seesaw, as muscle tissue wastes away from a lack of essential nutrients and is replaced with fat tissue. The resultant lowered metabolic rate makes it much harder to lose weight the next time round. After years of this kind of abuse the thyroid stops functioning properly. An unbalanced thyroid can result in a negative muscle-fat ratio, making it difficult to restore the metabolism to a healthy rate, and weight loss becomes almost impossible once this occurs. Cutting down your calorie intake will result in a breakdown of muscle as well as fat tissue, because the body consequently uses its own tissue as a source of food; muscle tissue is a source of protein and fat tissue a source of energy. The reduction in muscle tissue results in a lower base metabolic rate than before the diet, which means that each cell in the body will perform its duties at a much slower rate, since muscles need energy to function. The more muscle tissue you have, the higher your metabolic rate. The slowing down of the body's metabolism, due to a decrease in muscle tissue from your restricted diet, makes you put on weight more easily than before you started dieting, and usually in a larger quantity.

Fat tissue, in contrast to muscle tissue, serves no other function than that of storage and insulation, which does not require as many calories. So, 1 kg (2.2 lb) of muscle tissue will burn up more energy for its daily functions than the same amount of fat tissue. Not only that, but the muscle tissue will also be smaller in size than the same weight in fat because it is denser.

Restoring a balanced metabolism

It is hard to believe that the Western world of plenty can suffer from malnutrition, but as Adelle Davis explains in her book *Let's Get Well*, "Fat is only lost when energy is produced, therefore weight cannot be taken off until fat is efficiently burned, a process requiring almost every nutrient." So, the basic secret is to have an efficiently functioning body, and a balanced diet ensuring enough nutrients to maintain a healthy metabolism.

Most people think that metabolism means the process of burning fat. Yet the term includes all the chemical processes that take place in living organisms, resulting in growth, generation of energy, elimination of wastes, and other bodily functions related to the distribution of nutrients in the blood after digestion. You can see from this definition that metabolism basically means the process of life. A lack of even just one of the essential nutrients prevents this process from continuing normally. This interference eventually manifests itself in the form of various symptoms. Excessive fatty deposits and water retention are just two of the possible effects.

HERBS AND THE BODY

*"I gained weight because I really enjoy my food. My doctor warned
me to lose weight due to my high blood pressure and a history
of obesity in the family. I took one bottle of Natruslim and lost
5 kg (11 lb) two months ago which I have not put back on."*
Mrs P. Hendricks, Matroosfontein

Metabolism and the thyroid gland

A healthy metabolism is crucial. If you wish to lose weight it is important for every
cell in the body to function efficiently, and the metabolism is dependent on the
thyroid. One of the most abused organs of the body, the thyroid gland is highly
sensitive to pollution and stress, including emotional and dietary, so in today's
hectic lifestyle this organ takes a real bashing.

Because of its sensitive nature the thyroid usually becomes disordered.
Disorder here does not mean disease as it would in the medical profession
(where tests used by doctors can only identify a disorder when it has become so
severe that it requires medical intervention). When I talk about disorder, I mean
that an organ or system has become slow or congested so that it can no longer
function at peak performance level. The thyroid is almost always disordered in
people who are overweight, irrespective of whether it has shown up positive
in medical tests or not.

Proper thyroid function is dependent on a sufficient dietary intake of the scarce
mineral iodine, which is needed for the manufacture of thyroid hormones. These act
as messengers instructing other organs what to do, including how many of their
own hormones to produce. This means that if we lack iodine in our diet, or are
unable to absorb it from our food, all our other systems will start slowing down too.

Due to its scarcity in our diet, iodine was added to table salt to prevent any
deficiency disorders such as goitre (swelling of the thyroid gland). Today, however, doctors and the media advise us to cut down on salt in order to spare
our circulatory system from damage. Unfortunately, cutting down on salt also

23

reduces our intake of iodine which, in turn, can result in an iodine deficiency and consequently a disordered metabolism.

Herbs are able to treat both diseases and disorders, though a disorder is far easier and quicker to heal than a disease since it hasn't yet developed into any serious structural damage. A disorder can rapidly be remedied by using herbal remedies and correct nutrition, whereas a diseased organ requires complex long-term treatment, depending on how advanced the condition has become.

The most important herb in your weight-loss formula is bladderwrack, a species of seaweed which is very rich in iodine. Bladderwrack helps to regulate the thyroid gland which governs the metabolism. If you are preparing your own tinctures and cannot find bladderwrack, you can substitute it with any of the dried seaweed that may be found in most health shops or Japanese grocery stores, since all seaweed is rich in iodine.

Detoxification and the liver

Detoxification is an essential process in any effective permanent weight-loss programme. It is better to lose weight slowly so that the breakdown of fat and the release of stored toxins in the body happen gradually. If this is done you should not experience any unpleasant symptoms. So, don't go on a crash diet when you begin using the herbs, take the herbal formula while eating your normal diet. A week or so after starting the formula your appetite will decrease naturally, and you can cut down on your intake. Your body will be telling you that you don't need to eat as much as before. If you follow this guideline you will no longer have to battle with yourself about the quantity of food you consume.

The liver is one of the most important organs in the body and, like the thyroid, it suffers constant daily abuse. The liver is a storehouse holding 13 percent of the body's total blood supply at any time, as well as sugars, fats and vitamins. It filters the blood, removing all impurities, helps to control blood clotting and also produces sex hormones. Bile produced by the liver and stored in the gall bladder, is vital for the breakdown of fats. The liver also breaks down complex proteins, fats and carbo-hydrates, and synthesises various types of protein required for the growth and repair of body tissues. Considering the above, if the liver is overburdened, the impact on the rest of the system is severe, resulting in repercussions throughout the entire body.

24

When carbohydrates are digested and absorbed, they circulate in the bloodstream as glucose. Insulin, a hormone produced by the pancreas, is released into the bloodstream and sends a message to the cells to increase their absorption of glucose, resulting in a reduction of the circulating glucose and a lowering of the blood sugar level. When blood sugar levels are low and no food is eaten to supply further glucose, the pancreas releases another hormone called glucagon, which activates the release of glucose into the bloodstream from glycogen stores in the liver. Due to its involvement in the metabolism of carbohydrates, the liver is also a major player in the regulation of blood sugar levels.

Hypoglycaemia, or low blood sugar, is a result of too much insulin being produced by the pancreas as a result of continual abuse suffered by the body in the form of diets that are rich in sugars and carbohydrates. Thyroid dysfunction, chronic stress, irregular eating habits and missed meals, nutrient deficiencies, drinking excessive amounts of coffee, tea and alcohol, cigarette smoking and certain medications produce the same effect.

A person who suffers from hypoglycaemia can get overpowering urges to eat. These urges can be so strong that, if food is not eaten soon, weakness, palpitations, panic attacks, nausea, dizziness, sweating and headaches may occur, as well as major mood changes such as irritability, hysteria and anxiety, which make it difficult to think and act rationally. These very real physical, mental and emotional symptoms cannot be ignored.

For hypoglycaemia sufferers, trying to cut down their food intake and lose weight is very disheartening because it is impossible for them not to eat when they are hungry – and if they do not eat they cannot behave normally. Hypoglycaemia is only now gaining recognition by the medical world as a real problem that needs to be addressed. In the past, the symptoms associated with low blood sugar were dismissed as being merely psychosomatic.

Taking herbs that help to regulate and heal the liver will, over time, reduce the unpleasant, periodic occurrence of distress from low blood sugar and once the whole digestive system is working well, the hypoglycaemic person will be able to behave normally around food, not like an addict needing a fix. Hypoglycaemia is easily controlled and remedied by the basic weight-loss formula.

The liver is also involved in inactivating hormones like oestrogens and steroids. A sluggish liver can result in a build-up of these hormones in the system. This is bad news for anyone trying to lose weight, because oestrogen, by its very nature and function, encourages the growth of fat. Hormonal imbalances are extremely common today, as a large percentage of women of childbearing age take the contraceptive pill, while post-menopausal women are frequently on hormone replacement therapies (HRT). If the liver is unable to process oestrogen and steroids, the following may result:

- enlargement of the endometrium (lining of the uterus)
- breast stimulation
- increased body fat
- salt and fluid retention
- depression and headaches
- interference with thyroid hormones
- increased blood clotting
- decreased libido
- impaired blood sugar control
- loss of zinc (important for immunity)
- retention of copper
- reduced oxygen levels in all cells, reducing their overall performance and resulting in general lethargy and malaise
- an increased risk of breast cancer
- a reduction of vascular tone, which may result in varicose veins and haemorrhoids

From the above list you can easily see that increased oestrogen levels and being overweight can be very closely linked. Therefore, if you are on any hormone medication, taking herbs to support your liver is essential if you wish to ensure that the hormones are properly eliminated from your body.

Furthermore, the liver plays a crucial role in the control of cholesterol levels in the blood. Cholesterol is produced by the liver, intestines and other organs and tissues, including the arterial walls, and has many functions in the body. Cholesterol is one of the building blocks of cell membranes and of the protective lining of the nerves, it is also necessary for the production of several hormones, including cortisol (responsible for the inflammatory response which kills invading germs) and the sex hormones, and lastly it is needed in the process of healing injured tissue, where it creates a protective coating. Excess cholesterol is returned to the liver for conversion into bile. A sluggish liver may not be capable of converting all the excess cholesterol into bile. This will lead to a build-up and deposit of cholesterol in the blood vessels, resulting in a thickening and hardening of the arteries.

It is impossible to lose weight safely and permanently unless the liver is healthy. If this organ is not functioning properly, a backlog of toxins cannot be removed from the system. These toxins need fat tissue for storage, which means that an increase in fat tissue is a direct side effect of excessive toxins in the system. If excessive toxins are allowed to circulate in the bloodstream they can cause a person to fall ill, as they interfere with the metabolism of every single cell in the body. Cells that come into contact with these substances are poisoned and damaged, as in any other scenario of toxic waste spillage.

Artificial sweeteners contain liver-damaging substances, so avoid foods containing them, as well as diet sodas. Even though they are marketed as a solution to weight control, they are damaging to your health and will negatively affect your weight-loss programme.

Dandelion is an important herb because it tones the liver and kidneys. Due to its regulatory effect on the liver it also indirectly helps to lower blood cholesterol levels. You might lose weight without healing the liver first, but you will feel tired, irritable and crave sweet foods. Before long you'll break your diet and put the lost weight back on again. So, decongesting and toning the liver will give you much better results in the long run. With a strong liver you'll have fewer cravings and bad moods and will feel so good that keeping your slim figure is easy, not a continual struggle.

Water regulation and the kidneys

Dandelion also regulates the kidneys, which help to flush out any excess water retained in your body tissues. This action also helps to break down cellulite which is caused by toxins and retained water. Unlike diuretic drugs, which remove potassium from the body, dandelion is a highly effective diuretic that is also a rich source of this mineral. Potassium serves many essential functions in the body:

- it promotes a regular heartbeat
- maintains the balance of water inside and outside the cells and body tissues
- regulates what passes in and out of the cells
- essential for normal muscle contractions as it, together with calcium and sodium, regulates the nerves that send messages to the muscles to contract
- maintains the normal function of the nerve cells, the heart cells, the skeletal muscle cells, as well as the kidneys and stomachjuice secretion

Because potassium does all of the above, it aids in the treatment of acne, alcoholism, allergies, heart disease and high blood pressure. Dandelion is an important ingredient in the weight-loss formula, as it will facilitate the breakdown of fat tissue and eliminate excess water.

Allergies and the adrenal gland

The adrenal glands produce hormones that are essential for keeping all the metabolic functions balanced and have to be in good health if you wish to have a slim figure. One hormone produced by the adrenals, aldosterone, regulates the sodium and potassium levels in the blood. This means that if they are not functioning as they should, you will probably be bloated from retained excess water.

Like the thyroid gland, the adrenals are deeply affected by stress because they produce the hormones responsible for the fight-or-flight response inherent in every mammal. When you are under stress, these glands release the hormone adrenaline which gears the entire body into action. When this happens continually, your system starts collapsing from sheer exhaustion. It is, therefore, useful to exercise in order to release built-up stress energies so that vital organs like your heart will not become overworked.

The adrenal glands also secrete the sex hormone progesterone. If you tend to become bloated before your menses it could be an indication that your adrenals are disordered. In this case it is a good idea to include the herb chaste tree to the basic weight-loss formula. Chaste tree is also useful for any menstrual irregularity such as excessive bleeding, irregular periods, painful periods, menopausal symptoms and premenstrual mood swings. It is a vital addition to the basic formula if you have put on weight after a pregnancy or since using the contraceptive pill.

Many people today suffer from allergies. One of the chief causes of this epidemic is a high stress level, which disorders the adrenal gland. The adrenals produce the hormone cortisol which causes inflammations in response to foreign protein in the bloodstream. If the cortisol secretion is suppressed or unbalanced due to anti-allergic medications (like cortisone) you'll need to use chaste tree to support the glands and regulate the secretion of this hormone.

I had numerous patients who couldn't lose weight, even though they had tried almost every weight-loss aid on the market. Once they began taking chaste tree in addition to the basic formula, however, the fat started melting away. This will be the case especially if you have gained weight since taking a course of anti-inflammatories, steroid treatment, or oestrogen medications.

Food processing and the digestive system

The digestive system is of major importance in any weight-loss programme. Because of the large amounts of non-nutritious starchy and fatty food we consume, like white bread, pasta, junk food and cakes, our colons become lined with waste matter. All these foods are mucus-forming.

The mucus in your gut is just like that in your nose: a slimy material whose function is to remove waste matter. Because the intestines become sluggish, a build-up of mucus lines the intestinal tract creating a perfect breeding ground for all sorts of microbes, including infestations of the fungus *Candida albicans*, which is now assuming epidemic proportions in affluent societies.

Absorption of the vital nutrients becomes difficult, if not virtually impossible, if there is no contact between the digested food and the wall of the intestine. Nutrients can no longer be properly absorbed through the intestinal wall due to this mucus barrier. So, no matter how nutritious your diet, it is still possible to develop a nutritional deficiency.

Constipation is another prevalent chronic complaint in the 'civilised' world. There are a number of causes of constipation, the most common being a lack of sufficient fibre in our diets. Medication such as iron tablets, certain anti-depressants, antacids and long-term use of laxatives can also cause constipation. You might suffer from constipation even though you have regular bowel motions. Often a tube of compacted faecal matter comes away the first time a person has colonic irrigation. Many people also suffer from diverticulitis (the formation of pouches in a weakened colon wall), which can vary in number and be large or small. These are perfect sites for the build-up of waste material. If you suffer from haemorrhoids or piles then you are also susceptible to diverticulitis.

The herb centaury stimulates the salivary, stomach and intestinal glands, increasing the digestive activity, and will, over a period of time, regulate the digestive system. This ensures a clean and efficient digestion so that proper absorption of nutrients can occur. Centaury also relieves constipation and gas. It is, however, not a laxative in the common sense and you will not suddenly get an urgent need to pass a bowel motion. Once the digestive system is healthy your blood sugar levels are regulated and all cravings disappear too. This and the reduction in appetite will be like a new lease on life for any dieter. Gone will be the internal battles with yourself because you won't have any overpowering urges to eat, instead you will experience the same hunger signals as any slim, healthy person. This will free both your mind and willpower, allowing you to put them to much more constructive use.

People who diet frequently generally have strong characters, but their power is turned inward, as they continually try to control their inner impulses. These powerful drives should rather be turned outward and channelled into creativity. If we spent the same amount of energy and attention we spend on our weight on our professions, hobbies or studies instead, we would all be high achievers. It takes an enormous amount of inner strength to fight these uncontrollable pangs of hunger, yet we manage to do it for extended periods of time. Concentrating on an external issue will take your mind off yourself and speed up the weight-loss process too.

Once you start taking herbs you must eat whenever you feel hungry. This does not mean you can pig out on junk food. If you are hungry, eat something fresh, nutritious and tasty, but not junk. Hunger is a sign that the body needs food. Don't ignore that. Just choose foods wisely. Soon you will be hungry less frequently, not because of strengthened willpower, but because the cells of the body are no longer sending 'eat' messages to the brain. You'll soon feel normal around food and won't have the urge to wolf down anything available.

Immunity and the lymphatic system

Another vital component, seldom mentioned but important, is the lymphatic system. This is the garbage disposal operation of the body and, if it is not working properly, your body will start operating like a rubbish dump with piles of waste (toxins) and lurking pests (germs) all resulting in disease.

The lymphatic system, part of the circulatory system, has to return fluid which has passed from the blood vessels through the tissues back into the bloodstream. The function of this fluid is to cleanse the tissue through which it passes. It contains cells that destroy any germs which may be lurking there. This is the honey-like liquid that oozes from sores and forms pus when infected. The lymphatic system is the backbone of our immune systems.

Cellulite is caused by a fluid build-up in the body tissues. Overweight people are prone to the formation of cellulite because of the sluggish circulation through their fat tissue. The only way lymphatic fluid can circulate is by indirect pressure exerted on the lymphatic vessels by the movement of the surrounding muscles. That is why, if you don't get much exercise (even gentle walking or housework), the fluid will remain in the tissues and start to build up. However, this fluid also contains toxins that have been removed from the cells between which it has passed. The effect of too little exercise, therefore, is a build-up of fluid and toxins in the fatty tissue, resulting in that ugly orange peel look called cellulite.

Cellulite isn't automatically removed by losing weight – you've probably seen a number of thin women with cellulite, often on their upper arms, thighs and buttocks. The reason for this is that lymphatic drainage (removal of excess fluid and toxins from the tissues) does not occur purely by decreasing the fat tissue. Detoxification and exercise are needed before cellulite is removed. Dieting does not necessarily detoxify the body, unless it is specifically designed to do so. Low-fat or calorie-restricted diets have no detoxifying effects whatsoever. Taking herbs is an excellent and easy way of getting rid of cellulite quickly because they facilitate the excretion of both excess fluid and toxins – the two causes of cellulite. This is why the herbal formula for slimmers is an excellent remedy for cellulite as well. It detoxifies and increases elimination by regulating the excretory organs such as the liver and kidneys.

You may have heard of lymphatic drainage massage, which is excellent for general detoxification and also gets rid of cellulite. By manipulation, lymphatic fluid is moved to the nodes for filtration; the lymphatic circulation is improved.

When you start on your weight-loss programme, it may be a good idea to have a lymphatic drainage massage two or three times a week for a month or so. If you are unable to seek professional help, replace it with 10 minutes of body massage with a loofah every night while immersed in a hot bath. Add half a cup of Epsom salts to your bath water to speed up the detoxifying effect.

Unbeknown to many of us the skin, together with lungs and kidneys, is one of the body's most important excretory organs, more so than the bowels. Therefore, activities that generate heat, dilating the pores of the skin and increasing perspiration, help to speed up detoxification. The best way to tackle cellulite at home is to follow these points stringently. You will not believe the improvement within two weeks!

- take the herbal formula for slimmers
- stop smoking
- be sure to eat a diet that is rich in fresh raw foods and stop eating all starches and artificial foods
- stop drinking tea and coffee
- have a hot bath every night; add half a cup of Epsom salts to the water and steep yourself until you feel a sweat break out; with a loofah sponge massage the submerged areas of cellulite for about one minute each

Another important feature in the control of cellulite is exercise which will increase the flow of circulation. Increasing the circulation throughout the body improves the metabolism of all the cells, letting them perform far more efficiently while speeding up the detoxification process.

HERBS FOR WEIGHT LOSS

*"I used to wear size 16 clothes and weighed 86 kg (187 lb).
After three bottles of Natruslim I lost 26 kg (57 lb)! I wear
size 10 clothing and my weight has remained stable at
60 kg (132 lb) for two years now."*
Sameeda Essop, Cape Town

BLADDERWRACK
(seaweed; kelp; black tang; cutweed)
Fucus vesiculosis

- rich in mucilage; helps to regulate the bowel, easing constipation
- rich in soluble fibre; lowers 'bad' cholesterol
- rich in iodine; helps to regulate the thyroid gland, this balances the metabolism and results in the burning up of excess fat
- kills bacteria
- boosts immunity, which results in the rapid healing of any infection
- lowers blood pressure
- protects against radiation
- rich in essential vitamins and minerals
- restores a flagging libido

"Kelp . . . is used in folk medicine to treat constipation, bronchitis, emphysema, asthma, indigestion, ulcers, colitis, gallstones, obesity, and disorders of the genitourinary (urogenital) and reproductive systems, both male and female. It is also claimed to 'clean' the bloodstream, strengthen resistance to disease, overcome rheumatism and arthritis, act as a tranquilliser, combat stress, and alleviate skin diseases, burns and insect bites." That's according to Varro Tyler, Dean of the Schools of Pharmacy, Nursing and Health Sciences at Purdue University, in his book *The Honest Herbal.*

33

CENTAURY

(gentian; feverwort; red centaury)

Erythraea centaurium

- revitalises, and improves performance and stamina
- helps to prevent excessive tiredness
- alterative and blood purifier
- heals ulcers and abscesses
- a bitter; improves digestion
- febrifuge
- aromatic
- gastric stimulant; facilitates the proper breakdown of food in the stomach
- a mild nervine; soothes and strengthens the nervous system which makes it useful for people that suffer from digestive problems due to stress.

Many people suffer from an insufficient stomach secretion of hydrochloric acid. This results in a condition which would indicate exactly the opposite, including symptoms like indigestion, gas and a burning pain in the stomach area. The herb centaury helps to relieve these unpleasant symptoms as it normalises stomach secretions.

CHASTE TREE

Agnus-castus

- tones the reproductive organs
- normalises and stimulates pituitary gland (especially progesterone function)
- alleviates acne caused by hormonal imbalances (better than hormone pills)
- normalises the sex drive
- helpful for premenstrual syndrome, relieves painful periods
- useful in menopause
- helps the body regain its normal hormone balance; if you wish to fall pregnant, take this herb for a few months after having stopped the contraceptive pill
- will induce weight loss in people who have put on weight due to pregnancy, the contraceptive pill, or after a course of steroids (including cortisone)

CLEAVERS
(goosegrass; barweed; mutton chops)
Galium aparine

- assists the weight-loss process as it promotes detoxification and excretion of excess water; excellent in combating cellulite
- lymphatic tonic; boosts the immune system and is useful for people that suffer regular infections and swollen glands
- alterative; facilitates proper action of all cells in the body, thereby promoting proper nutrient utilisation
- diuretic; promotes excretion of excess water and in so doing helps to lower blood pressure
- blood purifier; improves skin disorders, including psoriasis, acne and eczema
- helps to prevent the formation of kidney stones
- relieves bladder and kidney inflammations
- relieves cystitis and painful urination
- rich in vitamin C
- anti-cancer properties
- anti-inflammatory; relieves inflammatory conditions such as rheumatoid arthritis and allergies

DANDELION
(priest's crown; swine's snout)
Taraxacum officinale

- stimulates weight loss and the flow of bile
- has proven to be very effective in clearing obstructions of the liver, gall bladder and spleen
- tones the liver, modifying and increasing its secretions
- improves kidney and bladder ailments
- laxative
- helpful against yeast infections like *Candida albicans*
- lowers blood sugar

- rich in vitamins A and C and in the mineral potassium
- a powerful diuretic; very rich in potassium, which makes it a great aid in cases of water retention due to heart problems
- lowers 'bad' cholesterol and blood pressure
- an excellent general tonic
- rich in iron and useful for anaemia and general energy depletion

ECHINACEA
(cone flower; black Sampson; Rudbeckia)
Echinacea angustifolia

- nonspecific immune system stimulant
- cortisone-like properties, improves allergies
- antibacterial
- improves upper respiratory tract infections such as laryngitis and tonsillitis; also good for catarrhal conditions of the nose and sinuses
- relieves colds and influenzas
- useful in speeding up the healing process in hard-to-heal wounds and sores, abscesses, boils, gangrenous wounds, septicaemia and ulcers
- antiviral; useful in the treatment of herpes and influenza viruses
- anti-cancer and anti-tumour properties
- insecticidal; good as external application for spider bites

HAWTHORN BERRIES
(May; Mayblossom; haw; quick thorn)
Crataegus oxyacanthoides

- one of the best heart and circulatory tonics
- improves heart weakness, palpitations, high blood pressure, arteriosclerosis and angina pectoris
- gently normalises heart action, either stimulating or depressing its activity depending on the need

LIQUORICE
(*Liquirita officinalis*; licorys)
Glycyrrhiza glabra

- allows weight loss to occur by revitalising the adrenals after a course of steroid drug therapy
- improves adrenal gland function
- demulcent; soothes and protects irritated or inflamed internal tissue
- expectorant for coughs, respiratory congestion, asthma and bronchitis
- anti-inflammatory; relieves peptic ulcers and bladder infections
- laxative
- cortisone-like effect useful for allergies
- reduces blood and liver toxicity
- detoxifies potentially poisonous drugs and alcohol
- high mucilage content; reduces 'bad' cholesterol and lowers blood sugar
- useful for diabetics
- inhibits tumour growth
- reduces emotionality and irritability

OATS
(groats; oatmeal)
Avena sativa

- excellent in supporting the nervous system in times of stress
- improves mood, especially in conditions like depression, irritation, hysteria and anxiety
- soothes and supports the nervous system
- improves conditions of nervous exhaustion
- helps to induce sleep in people suffering from insomnia
- useful aid in breaking drug and alcohol addictions
- supplies essential vitamins and minerals
- blood purifier
- rich in mucilage, which helps to lower 'bad' cholesterol

CREATING THE FORMULA

Before you start

The formulas that follow are merely guidelines to get you started and may be adapted to suit your particular needs. However, before you start experimenting, some additional items are required and there are a few points to bear in mind:

- obtain a dropper bottle from your pharmacy so that you can easily administer the herbs in drop form
- herbs are usually sold in dropper bottles; you may choose to re-use these instead of buying further empty bottles
- all the herbs listed should be available from your local health shop – if they are not, you may also order them from Natruhealth (see page 93 for order form)
- carefully read through Chapter 6 (Herbs for Weight Loss) to gain an idea of the therapeutic action of each herb
- the four herbs contained in the basic formula (bladderwrack, centaury, cleavers and dandelion) should always be included
- you may add additional herbs that you think may be beneficial to you, but do not mix more than six herbs at a time, since the percentage of each ingredient will become so small that it won't have much healing effect on the organs it is supposed to regulate
- take 15 drops three times daily, 10 minutes before eating

How to prepare a tincture

A 30 percent (60 proof) alcohol like Vodka or Cane, obtainable from any bottle store, should be used as the base. Vinegar may also be used, though the vinegar-based tinctures don't last as long as the ones that have alcohol as a base. If you prefer using vinegar, keep in mind that cider vinegar is best as it, too, has healing properties (use dried herbs if working with vinegar).

- chop the herbs finely or grind with a pestle and mortar
- place 120 g (4½ oz) dried, or 240 g (9 oz) fresh herbs into an airtight glass container
- pour ½ litre (18 oz) of alcohol into the jar and close
- shake well and place in a warm place, but out of direct sunlight
- steep for at least two weeks, shaking the container daily; the longer the mixture is left to steep the more potent the tincture
- remove all plant material by straining through a sieve or cloth

THE BASIC weight-loss FORMULA

Decide on which percentage of each herb you are going to use according to what you feel your particular requirements and weaknesses are. If you are generally sluggish and know that your thyroid gland needs attention, use more bladderwrack than other herbs. A good start is to use equal amounts of the four herbs in the basic formula:

10 ml (2 tsp) bladderwrack
10 ml (2 tsp) centaury
10 ml (2 tsp) cleavers
10 ml (2 tsp) dandelion

WEIGHT-LOSS FORMULA
(ALLERGIES)

If you suffer from allergies, add liquorice to the basic formula.

10 ml (2 tsp) bladderwrack
10 ml (2 tsp) centaury
10 ml (2 tsp) cleavers
10 ml (2 tsp) dandelion
5 ml (1 tsp) liquorice or chaste tree

WEIGHT-LOSS FORMULA
(CARDIOVASCULAR PROBLEMS)

If you suffer from cardiovascular problems, be it high blood pressure, angina pectoris, or a high cholesterol level and related water retention, simply add a few hawthorn berries to the basic formula. It would also be a very good idea to add some oats because people with cardiovascular disorders are usually highly stressed individuals, and the oats will have a calming effect.

10 ml (2 tsp) bladderwrack
10 ml (2 tsp) centaury
10 ml (2 tsp) cleavers
10 ml (2 tsp) dandelion
5 ml (1 tsp) hawthorn berries
5 ml (1 tsp) oats

WEIGHT-LOSS FORMULA
(KIDNEY PROBLEMS)

If you have weak kidneys, tend to suffer from recurrent kidney infections, or retain a lot of water in your body, increase the amount of dandelion in the formula.

10 ml (2 tsp) bladderwrack
10 ml (2 tsp) centaury
10 ml (2 tsp) cleavers
20 ml (4 tsp) dandelion

WEIGHT-LOSS FORMULA
(LIVER PROBLEMS)

The signs of poor liver function are indigestion, difficulty in digesting fats, lots of winds, acidity, irritability, a craving for sweets or alcohol, and a sense of tiredness on waking in the morning.

If you know that your liver is not functioning properly, or feel that it may be congested, adding more dandelion and centaury to the basic formula will help to alleviate the condition.

10 ml (2 tsp) bladderwrack
15 ml (2½ tsp) centaury
10 ml (2 tsp) cleavers
15 ml (2½ tsp) dandelion

WEIGHT-LOSS FORMULA
(LOWERED IMMUNITY)
If you tend to get swollen glands and suffer from recurrent colds and flu or other infections, or if you have any wounds that are slow to heal, add echinacea to the basic formula.

12 ml (2¼ tsp) bladderwrack
8 ml (1¼ tsp) centaury
12 ml (2¼ tsp) cleavers
8 ml (1¼ tsp) dandelion
10 ml (2 tsp) echinacea

WEIGHT-LOSS FORMULA
(MENSTRUAL PROBLEMS)
Women who suffer from any menstrual irregularities, be they very painful periods, a bloated feeling or mood changes before the onset of the period, an irregular menstrual cycle, heavy bleeding, or menopausal symptoms, should add chaste tree to the basic formula.

10 ml (2 tsp) bladderwrack
10 ml (2 tsp) centaury

41

10 ml (2 tsp) cleavers
10 ml (2 tsp) dandelion
10 ml (2 tsp) chaste tree

WEIGHT-LOSS FORMULA
(STRESS)
If you tend to be very stressed, add some oats to the basic formula.

10 ml (2 tsp) bladderwrack
10 ml (2 tsp) centaury
10 ml (2 tsp) cleavers
10 ml (2 tsp) dandelion
5 ml (1 tsp) oats

WEIGHT-LOSS FORMULA
(THYROID PROBLEMS)
If you feel that your thyroid gland may be unbalanced, whether it be over- or underactive, add more bladderwrack. Signs of an underactive thyroid range from sensitivity to cold, forgetfulness, feelings of depression, difficulty in losing weight, a dry skin, lethargy, headaches, menstrual problems, frequent constipation, hair loss, a low libido and recurrent infections.

20 ml (4 tsp) bladderwrack
10 ml (2 tsp) centaury
10 ml (2 tsp) cleavers
10 ml (2 tsp) dandelion

EATING STYLE

*"I have already lost 20 kg (44 lb) in two months. The formula has
also helped in controlling my appetite. I now eat less naturally."*
Patricia Mothlagodi, Dinokana

What has become of us?

If we ate a healthy variety of foods including a wide range of fresh herbs, salad greens, vegetables and fruit, as well as good-quality meat and fish, and free-range chicken and eggs, we would have very little need for doctors and weight-loss aids. Almost all disease, including excess fat, is caused by some kind of deficiency. Even eating too much can lead to nutritional shortfalls – strange, but true! Constant supplies of masses of food leave the digestive system with no time to rest. And, like everything else, if it is overworked it will break down, meaning that food cannot properly be broken down and absorbed. This leads to nutritional deficiencies.

Today, many of us have unhealthy digestive tracts due to the large amounts of junk food in our diet. Diets high in starch and dairy products lead to excessive mucus production, which after a period of time can build up along the intestinal walls. The accumulated mucus lining becomes a favourable breeding ground for unhealthy organisms such as the fungus *Candida albicans*. Furthermore, the unhealthy lining now forms a barrier between the eaten and digested food and the gut wall, preventing the proper absorption of nutrients. This in turn leads to a nutritional deficiency which then spirals into a malfunctioning physiology, creating further nutritional shortfalls.

I'd like to talk a little more about *Candida albicans*, a much-debated issue among medical professionals. Infestations of this fungus have assumed epidemic proportions in the Western world and are very closely linked to a lowered immune system as well as chronic fatigue syndrome. You might ask what this has to do with weight loss. If you have a Candida overgrowth, it not only causes excess weight, but is also responsible for many of the food allergies and digestive problems which exacerbate the difficulties inherent in losing weight.

The human body harbours over 400 different species of micro-organism in the nose, ears, mouth, colon and reproductive system, which produce essential chemicals needed for the biochemical processes taking place in the body. These organisms are incapable of producing disease in healthy human beings because sophisticated internal systems, like the immune system, maintain an ecological balance (homeostasis).

The body is subjected to many stresses like pollutants (cigarettes, industrial smoke and exhaust fumes), toxins (preservatives and drugs), emotional upheavals and extremes of temperature. Our bodies need to adapt to these influences, and what we call symptoms of disease are actually signs that they are readjusting. A bout of diarrhoea, for instance, is the elimination of dead bacteria, broken-down blood, bile and other materials. Contrary to popular belief, the intestinal system is not a major avenue for eliminating waste from the body, but serves to flush out toxins released from the cells.

Stopping the symptoms does not mean that the cause of the disease has been eradicated, it means that the illness has been suppressed. Though the symptoms have been alleviated or may even have disappeared, the person's energy will be low, and the vitality and enthusiasm present before the treatment no longer evident. Then, as often happens, the symptoms return after a period of time, or if they have been severely depressed, a new and often more serious disease develops.

Bowel bacteria are essential for the development of a normal immune system. They also synthesise vitamins, mostly of the B group, and including vitamin K. Most importantly, there appears to be a relationship between the permeability of the gut mucous membrane (lining) and normal bowel flora (bacteria). If the flora becomes unbalanced, as occurs from antibiotic treatment, the gut membrane becomes abnormally permeable, rather like a sieve in which the holes are too big, allowing for the absorption of inadequately broken down proteins and the reabsorption of toxins from the bowel content. This is one of the explanations for the large increase in food allergies prevalent today.

The resultant high toxicity levels in the circulation system lead to an increased strain on the liver and to various symptoms. Abdominal swelling, flatulence, and disordered bowel habits like diarrhoea and constipation can eventually lead to irritable bowel syndrome, a spastic colon, ulcerative colitis and Crohn's disease. These adverse side effects may not start for several days or even weeks after stopping antibiotic therapy, so that the relationship is often not obvious.

Below follow just a few of the side effects, listed by the *Monthly Index of Medical Specialists*, that are directly linked to disorders treated with antibiotic substances:

- nausea and vomiting
- skin rashes
- gastrointestinal disturbances
- neurological reactions include inflammations of the optic nerve
- inflammation of the tongue
- haemolytic anaemia (the shortened lifespan of red blood cells, and the inability of the bone marrow to keep up with the replacement of fresh cells)

Until recently, bacteria were considered the first and foremost causes of inflammations. However, bacteria fulfil an important biological duty. They secrete an enzyme which sets free stored toxins, and it is these toxins which cause inflammation. The inflammation actually plays a very important positive role, as high temperature, in turn, destroys viruses and other harmful elements, which are then eliminated by the pus, suppuration and mucus.

This is why it is very important not to suppress these discharges, otherwise the toxins are blocked inside the body and lead to further illness. Once the toxins are eliminated, the bacteria are no longer useful and disappear, leaving the body healthy and free of toxins.

When this biological process of reconstitution is interfered with or interrupted by antibiotic treatment, the body is not able recreate its tissue in a healthy fashion, which can lead to chronic illnesses such as immune deficiency diseases and Candida infestation.

Affluent societies pamper their bodies. We are overcautious when it comes to our health and smother our bodies by giving in to their every whim. When we are hungry, we eat. We have become experts at instantaneous gratification. Everything must be done as soon as we feel the need – fast foods, fast cars, immediate communication with anyone anywhere on the planet. Take someone used to this lifestyle and put them in the bush for a week and they wouldn't survive three days.

Do you remember the last time you went without food for two or even just one day? We panic when we don't know where the next meal is coming from. This is not natural. Our forefathers had to hunt for their food and, when they were unlucky, had to go without. Our bodies, too, are strong enough to survive a few weeks without any nourishment.

What happens when we get a fever or cold: we rush off either to the doctor or to the pharmacy and get some medication to stop the symptoms. This is gross abuse of the body's natural ability to heal itself and basically boils down to our fear of pain and death. Our bodies are incredibly strong and able to survive most of the hardships they may encounter. We are responsible for making our bodies weak by overprotecting them.

The same applies to children with overprotective mothers: they become smothered and develop asthma. The body's symptoms are an accurate expression of resistance to any unbalancing influence. The more we suppress these symptoms the weaker our bodies become, and we end up with chronic conditions like cancer, heart problems and immune-deficiency diseases. We have to start trusting that our bodies can cope. You must be prepared to experience some discomfort, because at the end of the painful period your general health, as well as weight and wellbeing will improve dramatically. Louise Haye's book *Love Your Body* is an excellent guide to the possible mental and emotional counterpart of most illnesses, including being overweight. Often, understanding the emotional side of excess weight can be instrumental in shedding fat that has tenaciously resisted any previous attempts at reduction.

Our food provides all the medical help we need

Before the advent of modern medicine, mothers were responsible for nursing ill family members back to health. This is why so many of the so-called folklore remedies are really effective.

A large percentage of our modern drugs are based on traditional medicine. Researchers journey to remote rural villages to discover what plants are being used medicinally. They then take samples of these back to the laboratories where the active ingredients are removed and used in large doses. The problem with this method is that using only part of a plant does not have the same healing effect on the body as using the entire plant would have. Concentrated, isolated active ingredients are often toxic, a fact often used by scientists to discredit herbal therapy. It is important to use the whole herb because it contains synergistic elements that naturally neutralise the poisonous effects of any toxic constituents it might contain.

All the food we consume has a physiological effect on the body. Fresh, unprocessed food contains a whole range of substances from enzymes to vitamins and carbohydrates. All these are either building blocks or catalysts for metabolic processes. A poor diet will result in a faulty metabolism and a lack of the necessary substances essential to repair and rebuild our bodies.

By diet I don't mean a calorie- or fat-reduced diet. I am talking about the art of eating food. Choice of food and the method of preparation used determines our basic health. So when I talk about food, I mean the healing potential that it contains at the same time. Junk food is literally poison, because it is denatured as a result of the processing and manipulation it goes through to create its taste and appearance. If we knew how to prepare tasty nutritious food we wouldn't enjoy the taste of junk food. Few would prefer eating a hamburger over a delicious meal prepared by a gourmet chef.

Tasty food does not have to be bad for you. It is all a question of skillfully learning to combine foods with an array of herbs and spices that tickle the taste buds. The more you practice, the better you'll become. The following chapter lists a variety of everyday foods, and their properties, that should be included in your diet. Use these foods as much as possible and create new ways of preparing dishes including these ingredients.

In our not-so-distant past, herbs were not only eaten when a person was ill, but were included in the everyday diet. The plants gathered for food had a wide range of tastes and effects on the body. Taste is a good indication of what the food is good for. For example, bitter foods are good for the digestive system, sweet ones give added energy and sour foods are toning.

The fare available at supermarkets is very limited compared to all the food actually available in the world. God created so many different leaves, branches and trunks, as well as roots and herbs that have since been eliminated from our diets through a process of selection. We discarded the foods we found unappealing and only cultivated what we found tasty.

'You are what you eat' is the modern-day version of 'let your food be your medicine, and your medicine your food'. Because we are eating weak foods, we become more vulnerable to disease. When you compare ginseng to a carrot, you will find that ginseng is much hardier. Ginseng is used very successfully as a tonic and aphrodisiac and also boosts the immune system. It grows in harsh mountainous regions, yet can survive for more than 1000 years. In sharp contrast, a carrot grows only in temperate climates and its life span is about three months. If you do not eat it within three months it will decay and disappear. Herbs give everlasting strength, whereas regular foods only supply temporary nourishment.

The foods we commonly eat and enjoy are also relished by the germs in our bodies (especially junk food). Germs utilise food to maintain their lives as we do. Fortunately herbs do not nourish germs and human beings equally. Humans, exercising their willpower, are able to eat distasteful herbs. Germs, not being blessed with willpower, are repelled by them. When human blood contains herbal nutrients (phytochemicals), the germs will starve to death and the human body will be cleansed and purified. The cleansing and purifying properties that allow herbs to survive for years without rotting are the greatest benefits to be gained from including these plants in your diet.

Relish your food

If the body is deprived of food for any length of time the metabolism slows down since it assumes that food is scarce. And, due to the fact that your body is excellent at adapting to new circumstances, it will quickly adapt to a reduced calorie intake. However, once you begin to eat normally again, either because you are fed up with being continually hungry, or because you have lost what weight you wanted to lose, you will put the pounds back on again since the quantity of food that you revert to is now too much for the slower rate of metabolism your body has developed.

What you need to do, is to change the whole way in which you perceive food and diet. Don't think about calories or fat grams, rather think about quality. How many nutrients and healing properties does your food contain? Is it fresh, tasty, and rich in natural colour? Why not add herbs, mustard, soya sauce, cider vinegar or a little garlic to your dishes? All of these contain nutritious and healing substances.

In addition to their indisputable healing benefits, the so-called condiments also add flavour and variety of taste to food. When a dish gives off a good aroma it automatically starts the digestive juices flowing freely.

Just imagine a juicy steak! Let your mind drift, and imagine the aroma, the taste and the texture of the dish. Your mouth starts watering at the mere thought. This is good because the digestive juices thus produced will break the fibres of the meat down quickly and efficiently so that all the amino acids can be utilised.

A completely different scenario occurs when you have to eat some diet food that you don't find appealing at all. Imagine eating a fat-free, sugarless muffin – it is stodgy and difficult to swallow because you can't muster enough saliva to wash it down. Its fattening cousin of the buttered, sweet variety, however, is very easy to gobble up. Saliva flows readily to get that delicious morsel down to your stomach.

So, the trick is to create meals that are delicious as well as healthy, meaning both easy to digest and full of healing properties. When you begin your weight-loss programme, do not drastically cut down your food intake. Three meals a day, a plateful at each sitting, and two snacks in between are the normal amount of food your body requires. If your system is working properly and you are eating well, you will maintain a slim figure while eating this quantity. Of course, the food should not be overly fatty or sugary. In other words, what you eat should always be healthy, tasty and nutritious.

EATING RIGHT

*"I have been on this formula for a week and have
lost 2 kg (4 lb). I am very happy."*
Mrs E. Hager, East London

What we should eat

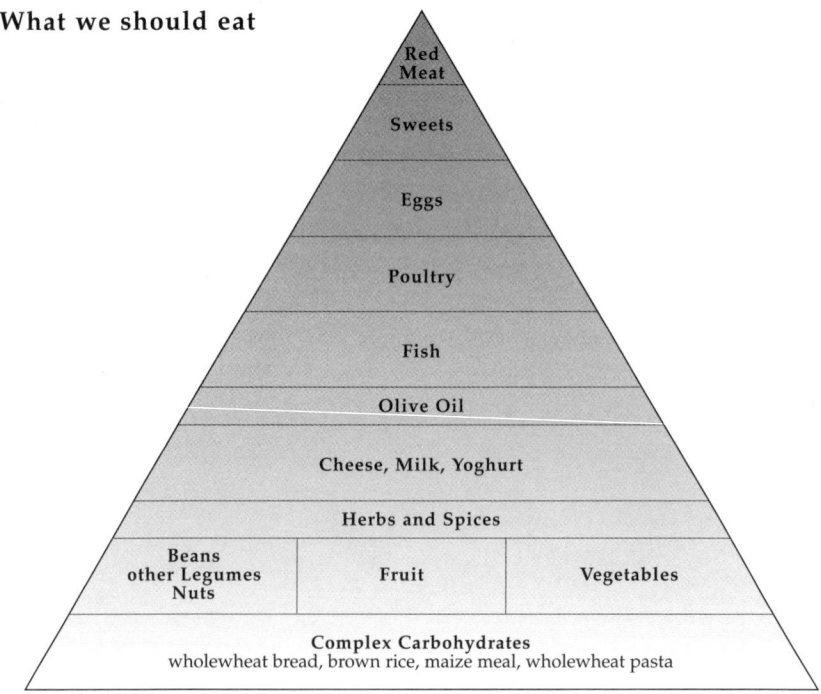

The above is the Mediterranean Food Guide Pyramid, which is a useful guide to choosing the proportions of different foods while doing your meal planning. I have added my own section – herbs and spices – as I feel these should be an essential element of our overall meal plan due to their powerful healing substances. Herbs and spices add a variety of tastes to what might otherwise be bland dishes.

Complex carbohydrates – our staple food

(6 – 11 servings of complex carbohydrates should be eaten daily)

The key word to keep in mind when shopping for your staple food is 'wholesome'. Keep away from white, refined starch as it drains minerals and vitamins during the process of its digestion without adding any benefits. Processed foods only add empty calories to your diet. These harmful foods include potato crisps, doughnuts, pastries, white bagels, white rice, white bread and white pasta.

Eat bread that contains whole grains and seeds, like sesame and linseed. The seeds are full of vitamins and minerals, especially calcium. Whole grains are potent packages of the vitamin B complex, as well as other vitamins and minerals. Both whole grains and seeds supply fibre which is necessary for good bowel function.

Fruit

(3 – 5 servings daily)

Fruit is not only delicious, it is also an excellent source of unpolluted water due to its high water content and, furthermore, is rich in various essential vitamins (especially vitamin C), minerals and enzymes. Bananas, spanspek (cantaloupe), and oranges are loaded with vitamins, minerals, fibre and carbohydrates. One banana contains as much as 25 percent of our daily requirement of the mineral potassium. Raw fruit, especially paw paw and pineapple, supply enzymes that aid in the digestion of proteins. If you suffer from poor digestion, have one of these fruits after a protein meal.

Herbs and spices

(use in cooking or sprinkle sparingly over prepared food)

These do not supply energy or building materials but do contain healing plant nutrients. Adding herbs and spices to your food will make it more tasty, which encourages the digestive juices to flow freely, ensuring thorough digestion. Many herbs and spices are known to have anti-cancer, antiviral, antifungal, and antibacterial properties, and can even boost the metabolism or calm the nerves. See Chapters 6 and 10 for an in-depth description of the therapeutic effects of the various herbs and spices.

Beans, other legumes and nuts

(1 – 2 servings daily)

All of these are rich sources of fibre, necessary for a healthy colon. The soluble fibre in beans and legumes helps to lower the levels of 'bad' cholesterol. Beans and legumes are a low-fat source of protein and vitamin B complex. Nuts are a rich non-dairy source of calcium, as well as other essential vitamins and minerals.

Vegetables

A diet that contains a variety of fresh vegetables eliminates the need for vitamin and mineral supplements, because all you need will be supplied in a form that is easily absorbed by the body.

The most important vegetables are those belonging to the the cruciferous family, like pak choi (Chinese cabbage), broccoli, Brussels sprouts, cabbage, cauliflower, collard greens, horseradish, kale, kohlrabi (turnip cabbage), mustard greens, swedes, turnips, turnip greens and watercress. Cruciferous vegetables are rich in vitamin C and have potent cancer-fighting properties.

Tomatoes, celery, carrots, salad greens, radishes and squashes are all incredibly healthy and great for those of us who need to lose weight. They are low in fat, rich in fibre and nutrients, and have a high water content, which means that you can eat as much as you like without having to worry about putting on weight.

Vegetables should be cooked lightly so that are still crunchy when eaten. This ensures that nutrients are not destroyed by overcooking. Cut a variety of vegetables into thin strips or small cubes, and stir fry them using a little extra virgin olive oil and naturally brewed soya sauce – a meal that is delicious and nutritious. Add herbs and spices to the vegetables for flavour and a little extra virgin olive oil after cooking. Avoid butter and especially margarine.

Olive oil

Use only extra virgin olive oil as this is made from the first cold pressing and is packed with quality vitamin E, linoleic acid and other nutrients. If extra virgin olive oil is not available buy virgin olive oil. These oils are more expensive than ordinary cooking oil, but if you cut down on your total oil consumption, the cost will level out. It is better to spend a little extra on health-enhancing oil than buying a cheap variety that causes 'bad' cholesterol and cardiovascular disease.

Extra virgin olive oil is delicious. It is truly amazing that healthy foods are more pleasing to the taste buds than their unhealthy counterparts. Scraping a piece of wholewheat toast with raw garlic and adding a little olive oil makes a very healthy and delicious snack.

Cheese, milk and yoghurt

(1 – 2 servings daily)

Use cheese sparingly as it is mucus-forming, especially the hard yellow varieties which are high in fat and salt. Healthier options are ricotta and cottage cheese.

Milk is another food we would be much healthier without. In its natural raw state, milk is very nutritious. However, after all the processing that it has to go through in order to be sold to the general public, it has become highly detrimental to our health. Like cheese, milk is mucus-forming.

All the good things we hear about yoghurt pertain to the unflavoured, unsweetened variety, called Bulgarian yoghurt. If you do not like the flavour, add some fresh fruit. The health benefits of yoghurt come from the bacteria used as its fermenting agent, the lactobacilli family of bacteria. Sugar and preservatives kill off these bacteria, so you might as well not eat yoghurt at all if you eat the sweetened type. It has no health benefits other than supplying some dietary calcium. Read your yoghurt labels carefully and choose a brand that states 'contains live culture' on the label.

Fish

Fish is an excellent source of complete protein. Of course, fish fresh from the sea, lake or stream would be most nutritious, but frozen and canned fish also supply good nutrients. Best are cold water fish like salmon, tuna, trout, catfish, mackerel and shrimp, which are good sources of EPA or omega 3 fatty acids which help to reduce 'bad' cholesterol levels in the blood. EPA has also been found to be beneficial for some forms of arthritis and maturity-onset diabetes by improving the cellular sensitivity to insulin. Put fish on the menu in place of red meat and poultry – your health and weight will be better for it.

Poultry

Ask your supermarket for free-range chickens. Most of the chickens available today are raised in terrible conditions and fed fish meal and antibiotics which remain in their tissue and end up on our plates. Unfortunately, modern chicken farming methods have changed a potentially good source of complete protein into a harmful food. These days, however, people are more aware of unethical farming practices and are demanding free-range chickens. If your local supermarket doesn't stock them, speak to the manager and ask him to order them for you. Free-range chickens supply all the benefits of poultry without the toxic residues remaining in the ordinary battery-raised birds.

Eggs

Fresh free-range eggs are a wonderfood. The yolk supplies all the amino acids the body needs, in addition to many essential vitamins and minerals. Eggs have, in the past few years, received some very bad publicity due to their 'bad' cholesterol and the cardiovascular disease epidemic experienced by affluent societies. However, if egg yolk is eaten raw, or rather soft, its cholesterol is of the 'good' rather than the 'bad' kind. The body requires cholesterol as the basis of its hormone manufacture. A raw egg yolk daily will supply all the protein building blocks for strong hair, nails and muscles, as well as the hormones needed for a healthy metabolism.

The important points to keep in mind when eating eggs are to eat soft yolks only, and not to fry them. If your cholesterol levels are normal try the following: crack an egg and separate the yolk from the albumen (egg white). Discard the albumen, or keep it for cooking. Add a teaspoon of cider vinegar to the yolk without breaking it. Then throw it to the back of your throat and swallow in one gulp. This is an excellent insurance for a healthy constitution, and you won't need to eat any other protein for the rest of the day.

Sweets

A little sweetness in our diet is necessary as a treat and adds another taste that makes our food varied and interesting. Avoid refined sugar and all artificial sweeteners (see page 67).

Raw, unheated honey is the best sweetener to use as it contains nutrients as well. The occasional piece of cake or chocolate is also fine as long as you don't overdo it. Give yourself a weekly treat as it will make your weight-loss programme much easier to stick to.

Sugar has a profound effect on the body, which is probably why so many people get sugar cravings. Sugar is a drug that makes us feel good and also acts as a tranquilliser, relieves anxiety and stress, induces relaxation and sleep, acts as an antidepressant and boosts some people's concentration. We get hooked on sugar just as we get hooked on nicotine. It is incredibly difficult to give it up. So don't be too hard on yourself if you lapse into a sugar indulgence, just cut it out the next day and continue from there.

Red meat

This is another foodstuff that has received much bad publicity. The reason why red meat is bad for you is that it is usually high in fat and contains residues of the steroids and antibiotics that were fed to the animals. The best red meat to eat is venison (wild game) as it has a lower fat content and is drug free. Like sweets, the occasional piece of red meat will do you no harm and will satisfy the craving that many people have for red meat – just don't overdo it. One serving per week is sufficient. Make it a tasty, well-prepared dish so that you can relish the meal and it will keep the craving at bay until the next red meat meal in a week's time. Red meat is expensive, so the money you save from cutting down on your consumption can be invested in buying the better quality foods lower down on the food pyramid.

Mushrooms

Mushrooms are a very good source of zinc, essential for a healthy immune system.

WONDERFOODS

"I gained weight after having two babies within two years. I lost 4 kg
(9 lb) using one bottle of Natruslim, and felt particularly good too."
Mrs M. de Vries, Ellis Ras

What are wonderfoods?

Up until the industrial era people ate rather monotonous diets of staple food. Herbs were gathered mainly for their healing properties and prepared in the kitchen as medicine. As technology advanced, enabling journies to faraway countries, so too did culinary and medicinal horizons expand. Travellers to distant lands learnt of new plants and practices, trade in spices began and a demand was soon created. Herbs were no longer the tools of the healers only, but became widely popular.

Coffee, which was originally introduced to Western society as an exotic pep-up tonic, is now drunk regularly all over the globe. The origins of Coca Cola are similar. In the late 1870s, John Pemberton learnt of a miraculous substance that was chewed by the native Peruvians and Bolivians: coca leaves. These were purported to act as stimulants, an aid to digestion, aphrodisiac and general life extender, and were known as 'divine plant' by the Incas. It took a patent medical doctor and a creative entrepreneur to introduce us to Coca Cola, the most common soft drink in the world today.

This chapter lists some of the foodstuffs and condiments that were introduced from foreign countries and exotic islands by the intrepid explorers of earlier centuries. As they all have special healing properties, including them in your diet will improve your general health and, therefore, encourage your body to return to its normal weight.

ALLSPICE

- carminative
  aids proper digestion

ANISEED

- expectorant
  useful for bronchitis and persistent, irritable coughing
- anti-spasmodic
  relieves griping and intestinal colic
- carminative
  improves flatulence
- parasiticide
  external use of the oil treats scabies and controls lice
- aromatic

BANANA

- prevents and heals ulcers
  (try eating banana to soothe a painful stomach ulcer)
- lowers blood cholesterol
- rich in potassium, which helps to regulate the water balance of the body
  and, hence, is useful for high blood pressure

DRIED BEANS AND LEGUMES

- control insulin and blood sugar
- help to regulate the function of the colon and hence improve constipation
- useful in the treatment of haemorrhoids and other bowel problems
- contain phytochemicals that inhibit cancer
- reduce 'bad' cholesterol
- lower blood pressure
- contain omega 3 fatty acids, essential for a healthy immune system

BROCCOLI, CABBAGE AND THE OTHER CRUCIFEROUS FAMILY MEMBERS

- lower the risk of cancer
- rich in vitamin C
- other vegetables in the cruciferous family are: Chinese cabbage, Brussels
  sprouts, cauliflower, collard greens, horseradish, kale, kohlrabi, mustard
  greens, swedes, turnip greens, turnips and watercress

CARAWAY SEED

- carminative
  relieves gas in the digestive system and soothes an upset stomach
  (especially in children)
- expectorant
  helps the removal of mucus in the lungs (by coughing up)
  useful in bronchitis and bronchial asthma
- relieves menstrual pain
- increases milk production in breast-feeding mothers

CARDAMOM SEED

- sialagogue
  stimulates the flow of saliva which helps in the digestion of carbohydrates
- carminative
  soothes flatulent indigestion and stomach pains

CHILLI PEPPER

- general tonic
- specific remedy for the circulatory and digestive systems
- improves the mood
  the burning pain on the tongue and throat excites the brain to secrete
  endorphin which blocks pain sensations and induces a kind of euphoria
- expectorant
  excellent for the lungs; helps to loosen mucus in the lungs
  prevents and alleviates chronic bronchitis and emphysema
- decongestant
  unblocks sinuses and nasal passages
- regulates the blood flow
- equalises the heart beat
  strengthens the heart, arteries, capillaries and nerves
- helps to dissolve blood clots
- painkiller
- rich in vitamin C
- improves general energy and helps to ward off colds

CIDER VINEGAR

Use apple cider vinegar that looks brownish in colour

- rich in potassium
  lowers 'bad' cholesterol
- protects against strokes
- prevents muscle cramping
- helps to regulate the body's water balance
- helps to regulate blood sugar levels

CLOVES

- help to relieve nausea, vomiting and flatulence
- a powerful local antiseptic
- has mild anaesthetic properties
  especially useful for headaches:
  hold a clove in your mouth for 15 minutes for headaches
  very useful for toothache:
  press a clove against the offending tooth
  rub a little clove oil around the painful area

FISH

The best fish are coldwater species such as salmon, cod, tuna, catfish, mackerel, trout and shrimp. All of these are rich in the omega 3 fatty acids, which have the following effects:

- increase mental energy
- help to prevent cardiovascular diseases
  lower cholesterol and inhibit blood clot formation
- protect arteries from damage
  thin the blood
- help to alleviate inflammation in rheumatoid arthritis
- alleviate migraine headaches
- boost immunity
- combat early kidney disease
- may prevent cancer
- may help in the treatment of maturity-onset diabetes

GARLIC

- contains cancer-preventing chemicals
- good for the cardiovascular system
  thins the blood, reduces blood pressure, lowers 'bad' cholesterol
- boosts the immune system
- expectorant
  useful for respiratory complaints
  helps get rid of mucus in the lungs
- decongestant
  helps to clear nasal and sinus passages
- prevents and relieves chronic bronchitis, influenza and respiratory catarrh
- antibiotic
- anti-viral

GINGER

- very useful in treating nausea and vomiting
  helps in cases of motion sickness
- warms up the body
  especially if you have cold hands and feet
- improves circulation
- lowers 'bad' cholesterol
- soothes and regulates the pancreas, the organ responsible for producing
  insulin, which lowers blood sugar
- relieves a cough with lots of phlegm in the chest
- promotes stomach secretions which facilitate proper digestion
- useful for relieving indigestion, intestinal gas and stomach pains

NUTS

Avoid products such as peanut oil, which, unlike other nut oils, causes atherosclerosis (fatty deposits in the arteries). Furthermore, peanuts and peanut butter
are often contaminated by a mould that causes cancer.

- rich source of non-dairy calcium (especially almonds and sesame seeds)
  calcium prevents colon cancer and osteoporosis (brittle bone syndrome), lowers
  blood pressure, relieves cramps and helps to maintain a healthy immune system

- nuts lower blood cholesterol levels
- regulate blood sugar levels
- are a rich source of essential vitamins and minerals
- studies showed that nuts contain chemicals that prevent cancer in animals

OLIVE OIL

If at all possible, try to use only extra virgin olive oil which is made from the very first cold pressing of the olives and is therefore packed with many powerful healing substances.

The more refined the oil, the less healing its effect:

- a powerful weight-loss aid
  research shows that olive oil can help the body rid itself of many insoluble pollutants that may be stored in body fat
- one tablespoon of extra virgin olive oil negates the cholesterol-raising effects of two eggs
- rich in vitamin E
- a powerful anti-oxidant
  which makes olive oil the perfect food for keeping us young
- lowers 'bad' and raises 'good' cholesterol levels in the bloodstream
- thins the blood
- acts as a mild laxative
- generally improves health and quality of life and reduces susceptibility to diseases and illnesses

ONION

- a good addition to a slimmers diet
  helps to control the appetite by regulating blood sugar levels
  helps to get rid of excess water
- used throughout the world as:
  help against infections
  diuretic
  blood pressure reducer
  expectorant
  heart tonic

contraceptive

aphrodisiac

- blood purifier
- has a calming effect on the nerves
  relieves irritability and insomnia
- soothes coughs and bronchial troubles
- antibiotic
- has cancer-fighting properties

PARSLEY

- excellent addition to a weight watcher's diet
  reduces water retention
  promotes detoxification
- anti-oxidant
  rich in vitamin C
  aids the body's defence against environmental toxins
- useful in soothing menstrual pains
- a magical breath cleanser
  useful once you start eating health-boosting foods like garlic and onion

PEPPERMINT

- one of the best regulators of digestion
  stimulates the secretion of bile and digestive juices
  soothes stomach cramps and combats flatulence
- excellent for relieving morning sickness in pregnancy
- relieves the nausea and vomiting caused by travel sickness
- anti-viral
  protects against herpes simplex and influenza
- helpful in relieving migraines that occur with digestive disturbances
- a nerve tonic
  eases anxiety, tension and irritability
- excellent for painful periods
  relieves the abdominal pain
- improves the mood

ROSEHIPS

- one of the best natural sources of vitamin C
- excellent spring tonic
  improves general energy and vitality
- helpful for constipation
- strengthens the body's defenses against infections, especially colds

SOYA

Use the beans, *tofu*, *miso*, and naturally brewed soya sauce.

- promotes slimming by balancing the appetite
  regulates blood sugar levels
- the only plant source of low-fat complete protein
  excellent addition to a weight-reduction programme
- replaces oestrogen
  useful in female hormonal imbalances
- regulates the bowels and prevents constipation
- useful in all cardiovascular disorders
  lowers 'bad' cholesterol levels in the bloodstream
- prevents and dissolves gallstones

THYME

- aromatic herb
  complements meat and chicken and also has profound healing actions
- excellent remedy for cardiovascular ailments
  lowers arterial pressure
  increases heart rhythms
  lowers blood pressure
  helpful for angina pectoris
- a blood purifier
  increases resistance to infections and improves skin disorders
- anti-microbial
- good for influenza and coughs
- soothes nervous disorders
- relieves stomach aches

TOMATO
- rich in vitamin C
- good for indigestion and liver troubles
- relieves constipation and kidney disease
- lowers cancer risk
- prevents appendicitis

WINE
- red wine is the alcohol weight watchers should drink
- prevents heart disease
  recent research has shown that nations which drink red wine have lower occurrences of cardiovascular diseases than nations that do not
- kills bacteria and viruses
- raises 'good' blood cholesterol
- garlic acid in wine is anti-carcinogenic (cancer producing)

YOGHURT
The health-giving properties of yoghurt are due to the lactobacilli family of bacteria used to ferment the milk. Sweeteners and preservatives kill off these bacteria, so eating sweetened, preserved yoghurt will have no health benefits. Make sure the label reads 'contains live cultures'.
- restores balance of healthy bacteria in the colon, especially useful after antibiotics have killed off both the good and the bad bacteria
- lowers 'bad' blood cholesterol levels
- prevents and treats intestinal infections, including diarrhoea
- regulates bowel motion
- relieves constipation
- boosts the immune system
- contains compounds that prevent ulcers
- has anti-cancer properties

FOODS TO AVOID

*"I lost 20 kg (44 lb) using three bottles of Natruslim, and
felt light and energetic. I continued losing weight even
after I stopped using the formula."*
Jean Marais, Cape Town

Foods can secretly poison

Unfortunately, technological progress is a double-edged sword. Large manufacturing plants situated close together create enormous amounts of concentrated pollutants. These have to be dumped somewhere and, invariably, they end up in our streams, seas, and land, before making their way into our bodies via the food we eat.

There is no way of telling whether our food and water are contaminated unless we have them tested in a laboratory, so we have to place our trust in the relevant government bodies to protect us from harmful substances. Yet, time and again, we hear frightening reports of excess pollution causing health problems among the population.

The governmental agencies that are supposed to protect us are also subject to economical pressures. Manufacturers have their own scientists declare the safety of their products, while on the other hand, independent researchers with no vested interest condemn pollutant levels as unacceptable.

The only way to safeguard our health, is by trying to buy organically grown foods as much as possible. Yes, these foods may be slightly more expensive, but rather spend a little more on food and save a lot on medical bills.

A quote from David Steinman's book *Diet For A Poisoned Planet* really sums up the entire problem of poisonous foods:

"In April 1985, signs appeared at piers and on the beaches of the county of Los Angeles: WARNING – EATING FISH CAUGHT IN SANTA MONICA BAY MAY BE HARMFUL TO YOUR HEALTH BECAUSE OF CHEMICAL CONTAMINATION. YOU SHOULD NOT EAT THE FISH CALLED WHITE CROAKER, KING FISH OR TOM COD.

I was shocked. I'd been eating locally caught sport fish for years. I wanted to know more. How dangerous were these fish? Was I going to die from having eaten them? It was pretty upsetting. I felt like a victim.

Newspaper reports eventually revealed that DDT-laced waste sludge from a pesticide manufacturing plant had for years been dumping in the area of Santa Monica Bay. To keep the barrels containing waste from floating and creating navigation hazards, barge workers hacked them open before dumping them. The contents of those barrels had accumulated in the bodies of fish feeding in these waters for years. Now they were accumulating in the bodies of people eating those fish.

At the time I was writing for the *L.A. Weekly*. I persuaded my editor there to support me in doing a study with a completely new approach by testing the blood of people who ate a lot of locally caught sport fish. My aim was to find out just how dangerous the fish were.

The answer was even worse than I expected. People who ate a lot of sport fish had serum DDT and PCB levels six to ten times higher than people who did not. I had my blood tested, too. Taking my age into account, I had one of the highest levels in the study group.

This news stunned me, as you may imagine. It started me wondering how many other poisons were in the foods I ate. It started me asking why government officials, who had known about the dumping for years, had withheld the information so long. It started me doing the research which eventually became this book."

It is not in the scope of this book to go into this subject in more depth. Read David Steinman's book (published by Ballantine Books in New York in 1992) if you wish to find out more about choosing safe foods for you and your family – it makes very interesting, if horrifying, reading.

Potentially healing oils become damaging fats

It is important to have a daily supply of fat in your diet. The advent of the low-fat diet craze persuaded some people to cut out fat altogether. A completely fat-free diet, however, has serious health implications. The body becomes deficient in the fat soluble vitamins A, D and E, which are essential for many physiological processes, one of them being immunity. If you lack fat in your diet you will begin to age rapidly, your hair and nails become brittle and skin disorders occur. A lack of fat can also result in increased allergies. So, whatever you do, don't cut out fat completely.

Confusion reigns regarding oils and fats. Which is better, butter or margarine? Not long ago, health experts told us to stop eating butter and use margarine instead if we cared about our cardiovascular health. Recently they have changed their opinion and now tell us that butter is better. In the meanwhile, most of us have resorted to avoiding all fats as much as possible.

Fats can play an important role in actually lowering 'bad' cholesterol and increasing the 'good' cholesterol which is health enhancing. A good quality, unrefined oil can strengthen your resistance to pollution and the diseases it creates within the body. We have to choose carefully, however, as most of the oils available in supermarkets are full of pesticides and are toxic due to hydrogenation.

Hydrogenation is the name of the processing procedure that is applied to unsaturated fats, like sunflower and canola oils, to make them semi-solid saturated fats. Margarine is a prime example: if it were not put through the hydrogenation process, we would have to pour it onto our bread. Hydrogenation also occurs when oil is heated, for instance, during the frying process. This is why fried foods are so bad for the cardiovascular system. It is not the oil itself, but the hydrogenated oil that causes the damage. Hydrogenated oil is as harmful as saturated fat, which can cause arterial deposits and atherosclerosis.

Unrefined oils, on the other hand, contain phytosterols which actually help to reduce 'bad' cholesterol. The beneficial substances contained in unrefined oil are altered by the hydrogenation process, thereby changing a potentially healing food into a harmful substance.

Quality cold-pressed oils are a rich source of nutrients. The best to use is extra virgin olive oil, which is made from the first cold pressing of the olives. Out of all the oils tested in David Steinman's book, it contained the least pesticides. Cold-pressed oil remains stable when heated, which means it does not become hydrogenated.

Other good oils are linseed, sesame and canola. Steer away from margarine completely. Not only is it harmful due to being hydrogenated, it is also full of chemicals and pesticides. Use butter instead of margarine, but in small quantities. Try a little extra virgin olive oil on bread – it is delicious and very good for you.

Artificial sweeteners are dangerous

Aspartame, a common artificial sweetener that is sold under various brand names, is found in almost all diet foods and beverages, and is potentially one of the most harmful substances passed off as food on the market today. This aggressively marketed, dangerous substance is capable of producing painful symptoms, yet many think it is good for them because of clever advertising techniques.

Many overweight people think aspartame will help them overcome their weight problem. Amazingly, increasing numbers of slim people have begun consuming drinks and food containing this harmful sweetener, thinking that these foodstuffs will prevent them from gaining weight.

Misleading advertising has resulted in millions of people willingly ingesting a toxic substance. The aspartame in beverages and food is absorbed directly into the bloodstream where it breaks down into its chemical components, one of which, methanol, is a poisonous alcohol. Symptoms caused by methanol ingestion include dizziness, headaches, numbness of the fingers, blurred vision, nausea, abdominal pain, hyperactivity, anxiety attacks, muscular and joint pains, loss of energy, menstrual cramps, ringing in the ears, skin problems, and a loss or change in taste. Methanol is also particularly damaging to the eyes and can, in some cases, cause blindness.

It is very important to avoid aspartame during pregnancy. Some of the children, born to mothers who used aspartame frequently during their pregnancy, were born without any eyes. These children also generally have lower IQ levels than children of mothers who did not use aspartame.

You may prefer to take your chances, and continue eating or drinking substances containing this artificial sweetener in the hope that they will help you keep your weight down, but in the long run the continued toxic effect of aspartame will put a strain on your liver, resulting in weight gain.

MIND OVER MATTER

"Not only did I lose 12 kg (26 lb) using the herbal formula, but my skin and hair improved as well."
Mrs J.C. Louwrens, Kenwyn

Think slim

Weight fluctuation is often a sign of mental or emotional distress – you are not happy about something in your life and are not confronting it. Usually a life situation causes an imbalance in the body resulting in weight gain. This can be anything from overwork to an unhappy relationship. If you lose weight, but don't change the way you feel, you will inevitably put the weight back on again after stopping the weight-loss programme.

The power of thought is an essential ally in creating the life and weight we desire. Everything around you began as a thought. To start a business or bake a cake you first plan what you are going to do (thought) and then put the plan into action. In order to create anything you have to give the project a lot of thought before and during its development. Similarly, you need to keep your goal weight in mind and imagine how you are going to achieve it.

Before you begin your weight-loss programme, draw up a plan of what changes you are going to make in your life. Revise this plan as you go along. Delete the things that don't work for you and add new ideas as you think of them. Be flexible. If one form of exercise doesn't suit you, start a different training programme. Don't think of yourself as a failure if you don't stick to the original plan, all things are created by trial and error. Eventually you will fine-tune your programme into one that works well for you.

A useful tool for achieving your goal weight is visualisation. In your mind's eye imagine what you will look like when you have achieved your ideal weight. Imagine what your life will be like. Most of us feel unworthy, guilty and ashamed of ourselves because we are overweight. People can be nasty and may talk about us behind our backs. We have to ignore other people's negative behaviour and put our own negative feelings firmly behind us. If negative thoughts and feelings used to be our reality, we can choose a different, positive reality in which we feel beautiful and happy. This is what you have to see in your mind. Picture yourself happy and slim, and surrounded by supportive friends who respect you. See yourself as you would like to be and it will only be a matter of time before you become that image.

Visualisations should be done daily. Try and do them at a regular time. Find a place where you will not be disturbed, listen to some soothing music and relax. Clear your mind of all the stresses and negative feelings of the day, and concentrate on your breathing for a few minutes. Once you are completely relaxed begin your visualisations. Fifteen minutes daily is sufficient. If you can't find the time to do them during the day, a good time is at night while lying in bed before dropping off to sleep.

It is not easy to keep our minds focused on who we are becoming, rather than who we were. It takes practice and perseverance. The trick is not to give up when you experience a setback. Just tell yourself the binge you indulged in was a necessary release, and get right back onto the programme once again. Do not lose motivation and berate yourself for being weak. We are human after all, and letting ourselves go now and again is good for the soul.

Taking the herbal formula three times daily is a very useful regular reminder of your commitment to become slim and attractive. Each time you take the herbal drops you are connecting with your goal. You remind yourself three times a day that you are on the path to fulfilling your dreams – dreams of beauty, health, attractiveness and joy.

Your life changes when you become slim after having been fat. People start to notice you and are friendlier. You will receive sexual advances from the opposite sex. You will no longer be invisible, hiding behind your fat shield, and won't be able to blame your failures on your weight. You will have to take full responsibility for your life. Are you sure you want to change things? If not, you will continually sabotage your own weight-loss progress. Not, as is commonly thought, because you are weak and lack willpower. The reason for breaking your programme is that deep down you do not really want to be thin. I know this sounds shocking and unbelievable, but I've seen it over and over again. We may consciously think we want to lose weight (and who in their right mind wouldn't?), but subconsciously we need that fat as a shielding barrier.

Society does not let us get away with being fat. So, we may not feel too comfortable when we bend over to tie our shoelaces or can't fit into slinky jeans, but to some people this is not the end of the world. However, when we mix in society and receive the repulsion that seems to be reserved for fat and physically deformed people, we start to get the feeling that maybe there is something wrong with us. And since we all want to be liked and accepted we think we had better lose the excess bulk. This results in a need, not a desire, to lose weight. There is a difference, albeit it a subtle one. We don't necessarily want to lose weight but we do want acceptance, and the way to gain it is to become slim like other people.

Here is one of many examples of a subconscious need for excess weight: Sarah and George are happily married and have an active social life. Their first child is born, which means that certain social adjustments have to be made. Sarah can no longer go out in the evenings as she needs to look after their child.

After a short period of being the proud father, George becomes restless and wants to go out like they used to before the arrival of their son. Sarah is split between her duty as a mother and love for their son, and the need to keep up with George. To keep him happy she tells him to go out without her, although part of her would love to join him. After this has happened a few times, it begins to put a strain on their relationship. She feels that if he really loved her and cared about his family he wouldn't want to go out. She starts to complain when he comes home after having a night on the town. He makes amorous advances towards her in his drunken state and she feels anything but amorous. In fact, she feels resentful and angry. But if she denies him sex he might go looking for it elsewhere, so she relents.

As this pattern of behaviour continues, Sarah becomes increasingly upset with George. The way Sarah appeases her pent-up anger is by eating. At least the food gives her some pleasure and fulfilment. As she puts on more and more weight George stops finding her sexually attractive, which suits Sarah too, because at least she won't have to deal with his sexual advances when she is not feeling at all loving towards him. She is actually very offended and bitter and the only outward indication of this is her excess weight and the fact that she has become irritable and snappy. George, blissfully unaware, puts it down to the strange moods of women.

This is a terrible, yet common, scenario. You need to take a good, hard, honest look at your life to discover if there is any underlying unresolved feeling that your fat is covering up. Fat is very often a woman's defence mechanism.

So, when you begin taking the herbs and embark on your weight-loss programme, you must decide that you truly want to be thin. Once this is done you can make a firm commitment to your weight loss. When you imagine the impact that being slim will have on your life and you choose that life, you will have taken an important step on the path of permanent weight loss.

Louise Haye's book *You Can Heal Your Life* is a valuable guide for anyone wanting to fulfil their dream. It is possible. People all over the world are doing it. All you have to do is change the way you think. Release all your negative feelings about yourself and the world around you. It is difficult to succeed without undergoing emotional and mental change.

Another useful tool are affirmations. Affirmations are sayings that you repeat to yourself over and over. This is an effective way to train yourself to think positively. It is difficult to break the habit of self-criticism and feelings of worthlessness often experienced by people who are overweight. Saying your affirmations will train your mind to accept a new and different reality from the one you are in at present. Your affirmation should be a statement about who and what you want to be. It must be stated in the present tense as though it were already true. Some examples are:

- I am slim and attractive. Everything in my life happens for my greatest good.
- My life is fulfilling. I have a beautiful figure and I am comfortable in my perfect body.
- I am surrounded by love and joy. I attract all I need to ensure my happiness.
- I am a strong, powerful and beautiful woman.

Make up your own affirmations. Don't make them too long, capture the essence of your dream and write it down. Repeat your affirmations for a few minutes at regular periods throughout the day. Repeating affirmations to yourself is especially helpful when you are feeling low, or when someone is being horrible to you. Just shut out the world for a few minutes and repeat your personalised affirmations to yourself – or, if you are alone, sing or shout them out loud. Say them to yourself while looking in the mirror. They will give you the strength to continue on your quest for a beautiful, healthy body and a joyful life.

Whenever a negative thought pops into your head (and they are so persistent), change the thought into its positive form and repeat it to yourself several times. This will train your mind to think positively and keep you on track to achieving your goal. Some examples are:

Negative	Positive
• *I am useless*	I am strong and I strive through life's adversities.
• *I am ugly*	I am a beautiful person and I am surrounded by supportive and loving friends.
• *I am fat*	I am a unique and special person. I have a beautiful, healthy body.

These concepts may sound strange to those who have not come across positive thinking techniques before. Research has shown that most successful people use some form of positive affirmation. They become completely involved with their dreams, think about them often and imagine what their lives will be like once they achieve them. Their dreams are their passion, and because they invest so much time and energy in them, their behaviour is in accordance with achieving these dreams. Positive thinking works. If you're sceptical, try it anyway – you have nothing to lose except your excess weight.

THE PERFECT EXERCISE

*"Natruslim solved my water retention problem. I lost
5 kg (11 lb), I looked better and felt very good."*
Mrs J. van Tol, Hazyview

Walk yourself slim

By now, it is impossible to be unaware of the importance of exercise. But all the promoted regimes look terribly strenuous and exhausting – a chore rather than a pleasure. A lot of the participants in gym workouts (hailed as the answer to all our weight problems) look more like Herculean goddesses than normal women.

Is this natural? Of course it is not natural. The feminine body should be slim and soft. Women today are losing their femininity because they are trying to look like fashion models, most of whom have boyish figures. There is a difference between slim and muscular. Sure, if you have athletic ambitions or want to increase your strength, weight training and strenuous aerobics are the sports for you, but for most women who would just like to be slim and healthy, walking is ideal.

Walking is enjoyable, cheap, and sociable. It is great for body sculpting and, because it is low-impact, it is least damaging to your joints. Walking melts fat off the whole body – abdomen, hips and upper arms. The reason walking is fat burning is that it is aerobic. This means it increases circulation, oxygenation of the cells, detox-ification and metabolism. The areas of highest fat concentration melt away first.

Regular walks are the key to a firm, slim body. The pace needs to be brisk though, as your body will get very few health benefits from a slow, leisurely Sunday after-noon stroll. You will need to lengthen your stride, swing your arms and increase your pace. In order for walking to have any fat loss effects at all, you have to raise your heart rate and keep it at a raised level for at least half an hour. So, all it takes, is half an hour of your time every day, and you'll start to notice that your body is becoming slimmer and more toned within a few weeks.

Walking is good for the soul too. A walk in the woods, through a park, or along the shore will lift even the darkest of moods. Research has shown that exercise, including walking, is an effective antidepressant and helps to reduce anxiety, stress and anger. Walking off your anger is far more beneficial than focusing that destructive energy on revenge.

It has been shown that walking is more effective against cancer than extremely intense exercising. High-intensity workouts can actually increase stress on the body, which is detrimental to your health. I am sure many of you have heard of fit young men dropping dead from a heart attack while they were jogging. Rather take it at an easier pace, but for longer periods. The health and weight benefits will be far greater.

Before you start, make sure you have comfortable walking shoes with a cushioning sole. Sport shoe manufacturers are creating the most amazing footwear, some designed specifically for walking, that make you feel as though you were walking on air. Good walking shoes are your only expense, so splash out and get the best for your feet. You will reap the benefits in the long walk.

Early morning, when the air is fresh, the birds are singing and the world is still asleep, is the best time. If you cannot make it in the morning, any time you have a half an hour to spare is fine – during your lunch break, before sitting down to dinner or before going to bed. Unfortunately, many women are frightened of going out in the dark, partly due to the ever increasing crime rate. But walking at night under the moonlight is an uplifting experience – try it with a friend. Remember those romantic evening walks with your loved one? Recapture that feeling of freedom and joy, and walk and walk. Even a short walk around the block is fine if you don't have any natural environment close by. If you are unfit, walk as much as you can, slowly building up to half an hour. Take your children or partner along, they, too, will benefit from the exercise, while you'll spend some quality time together. You don't need any special equipment, so start today.

Be sure to wear a warm sweatshirt when you start out. Once you warm up you can tie it around your waist, so that you don't have to carry it and your arms can swing freely. Put it on again after your walk if the weather is cool. We are susceptible to the cold after a workout, because the evaporating sweat cools us down quickly when we are not moving to keep warm.

QUESTIONS AND ANSWERS

Is it safe to use herbs while on the contraceptive pill?

Many concerned customers enquire whether the herbs will reduce the efficacy of the contraceptive pill. Since the herbs that are recommended in this book are not stimulants, they will not impair the effectiveness of the contraceptive pill as conventional slimming tablets might do. Some slimming preparations have a reputation for rendering the contraceptive pill less safe. The reason for this is that they contain amphetamine, which artificially increases the metabolic rate. This means that the effect of the contraceptive pill will wear off sooner than expected and, if the dosage is not altered accordingly, pregnancy may occur. There is no danger of this happening when you use the herbs mentioned in this book.

Is it safe to use herbs while pregnant?

"My weight problems started after my last pregnancy. I lost 9 kg (20 lb) on Natruslim which I couldn't have done alone. I am expecting again and still taking the formula, and I feel great!" Shereen Hamman, Mitchells Plain

It is completely safe to use all the herbs listed in this book while you are pregnant. In fact, taking herbs during your pregnancy is extremely beneficial for yourself and your unborn child. Herbs detoxify the body and keep it regulated and healthy which means that the baby has a healthy environment in which to grow. The herbs also supply a lot of the essential vitamins and minerals needed for proper cell function. Nutritional imbalances and deficiencies can result in birth abnormalities, so taking herbs that ensure good health, vitality and nutrition will only ensure the birth of a healthy, happy baby. Anaemia and toxicity are two conditions that occur frequently in pregnant women. The basic weight-loss formula, which is rich in iron and encourages detoxification, will prevent these conditions.

Is the weight-loss formula safe for children?

"My eight year old daughter was overweight and lethargic. She lost 1.5 kg (3 lb) safely in a week, and became a normal, lively child again."   Jean Marais, Cape Town

Yes, the herbs are safe for children, although the dosage would need to be adjusted for toddlers (see Chapter 3, page 16). Herbs are extremely beneficial, no matter what your age. Overweight children very often become overweight adults, especially if obesity runs in the family. There are conflicting ideas regarding the reason for this phenomenon. Some researchers regard it as genetic, others say it is from learning the wrong eating habits at home. Whatever the cause may be, herbs will solve the problem.

An overweight child may suffer from a thyroid imbalance, even if medical tests have shown up negative. This has a profound impact on its intellectual capabilities and its immunity. Taking the herbs for slimmers will restore healthy function of the thyroid, resulting in a very different child. Its mood and intellectual ability in class, as well as its health, will improve dramatically. If you want to ensure your child's health and wellbeing, then putting it on herbs is one of the most beneficial things you can do as a mother.

Is it safe to use the herbs while breast-feeding?

Yes, it is completely safe to use these herbs while you are breast-feeding, although the texture of your milk might change during the first few days and your baby may, as a result, become slightly colicky. This is nothing to be concerned about, so continue using the herbs as before.

What is happening is that your body is detoxifying and regulating itself. The toxins released from the broken-down fat cells enter your bloodstream, as well as the milk on which your baby is feeding. However, your baby is already ingesting these toxins because your milk is rich in fats and therefore contains the same toxins that are stored within your fat cells. It is better, in the long run, to go through a few days of concentrated detoxification. Apart from helping both of you to detoxify, the herbs are also rich in essential vitamins and minerals which will ensure that your body is supplied with the building blocks necessary to produce nutritious milk of the highest quality.

Can people suffering from high blood pressure use herbs?

"I am sixty-eight and feeling great. I have more energy. My zest for life is back. My high blood pressure has stabilised. I was a size 42 and am now a size 38. My aches and pains are much less. Thank you for Natruslim – a great product." Mrs C.M. Mulligan, Kuilsriver

Herbs are especially useful in controlling blood pressure and are much more effective than any conventional hypertensive drugs on the market. I have had patients that were on hypertensive medication for years and still suffered from high blood pressure (hypertension). The condition was soon controlled once they started the herbal programme.

Herbs treat the cause of hypertension, they don't just force the pressure down – which could be dangerous, as the pressure is high for good reasons. For instance, if your arteries are clogged with cholesterol deposits there has to be a lot of pressure in order to pump the blood through to the extremities. If you force the pressure down you will begin to get cold hands and feet, and your energy will begin to flag. Men will experience impotency problems because erections occur when the penis becomes engorged with blood. This explains why impotency is a direct side effect of hypertensive drugs.

Although high blood pressure serves a purpose, it also puts severe strain on the cardiovascular system. High blood pressure needs to be lowered, but again, this should be done by curing the cause rather than the symptoms. Herbs effectively cure the cause of high blood pressure without the nasty side effects of conventional medicaments. If you are taking diuretics, it is very important to discontinue this medication because it has profoundly damaging effects on the body and will interfere with the action of the herbs. The basic weight-loss formula is a potent regulator of the body's water balance, so it is safe to substitute the diuretic with the formula.

Can underweight people use the herbal slimming formula?

This is not an uncommon question. People hear from friends how wonderful they felt from using Natruslim® and wanted to take it for its health boosting properties. The answer to this question is yes.

The basic formula for slimmers regulates all the systems of the body. This means it will encourage the body to achieve its healthy weight. Underweight people could put on weight using the basic formula, but I would suggest adding 10 ml (2 tsp) of oats to the formula. This nerve tonic will stabilise the nervous system which might be one of the weak points in an underweight person. Also, oats are a rich source of the vitamin B complex which is beneficial due to its regulatory effect on the metabolism.

Can I use the herbs if I am on thyroid medication?

"I was a body builder from the age of 18, but stopped going to the gym nine years ago. I continued eating as though still body building. During this time my weight soared to 133 kg (293 lb). I had a slight thyroid condition which also aggravated the problem. I took Natruslim regularly for three months and although my eating habits are not the best, I lost 25 kg (55 lb). My general health has improved and I feel good. The thyroid problem has completely disappeared." Mr Schneider, Phillipi

Yes, the herbs, especially the bladderwrack, help to heal the thyroid. If you have had a thyroid condition for many years, you will lose weight slower than most people. In the first month your energy and other bodily functions improve. You'll probably start losing weight in the second month, although some people on thyroxine have reported losing weight in the first month. As your energy and health improve, begin, under your doctor's supervision, to wean yourself off the thyroid medication.

It is possible that your condition can be cured with herbs, so persevere and slowly reduce the medication. People have reported goitre disappearing while on the basic weight-loss formula.

Often patients are told they will have to continue taking thyroid medication for the rest of their lives. This is very seldom correct. Unless you have had your entire thyroid gland removed, it is possible to restore it to some semblance of productivity. The thyroid is one of your most vital organs in the body, it produces hormones that are essential for the control of the function of every single cell. If you have been told it needs surgical removal, get a second, third or fourth opinion if necessary. Do not remove this organ, rather receive qualified holistic treatment. You will never be able to live normally again without your thyroid gland and will forever be dependent upon medication, which can become very costly.

Will I put on weight after using the herbs?

"I lost 5 kg (11 lb) in six weeks, and found that I continued losing weight even after I had finished taking the formula. My general mood improved too."   Mrs Lakey, Cape Town

Because you don't diet while taking the herbs, your body learns to adapt to a normal, healthy, balanced diet. Your appetite naturally decreases due to the blood sugar regulation and enhanced nutrient absorption. Weight is lost because all the organs in the body begin to function properly. This is why some people actually continue losing weight after stopping the herbs. Their body is cleansed and working efficiently, so it will continue losing excess fat until a healthy weight is achieved. Herbs are only necessary to regulate and detoxify the body. Once that is done it will lose weight on its own accord.

How can I be sociable and still eat properly?

"I would like to order another bottle of Natruslim. This will be my third bottle and like I said on the phone, I lost a lot of weight without watching what I eat. My friends can't believe that I lost so much. Do you also have responses like this from other users? You really do have a fantastic product. I first saw the advert in You magazine then I ignored it, but

after I saw it in the M-Net TV Guide, *I decided to give it a go and have not looked back. I also notice that there are no side effects which is so much different from all the other slimming products I used. "* Nthabiseng Julia Phafoli, Witsieshoek

Socialising, entertaining and healthy eating go so closely hand in hand that I am surprised this should ever present a problem. It is a pleasure to go out to a restaurant when you are on a healthy eating plan because you can just choose wisely from the menu, knowing that you don't have to spend time in the kitchen preparing your own meal. So make the most of dining out.

The first thing to remember is freshness and quality. Since the popular swing towards healthier eating habits, almost all restaurants offer salads on their menus. This makes the perfect starter. Order your salad without a dressing – no, don't panic, you are not supposed to eat a tasteless bunny dish. Just ask the waiter to bring some olive oil and vinegar on the side and you can quickly prepare a delicious and simple vinaigrette by adding a little salt and freshly ground pepper.

Do not eat anything starchy like bread, pasta, pizza or pastries. If you have to have pizza or pasta, eat them without cheese or any other protein.

Grilled fish, chicken or steak are fine. Do not worry too much about the size of the portions, rather be careful not to combine your foods badly. As a side order try some stir-fried vegetables, or any vegetables for that matter (do not add butter, but if they have added butter it's not too serious).

What is food combining?

Harvey and Marilyn Diamond have written an excellent book on this subject called *Fit For Life*. For a detailed description of food combining buy this book, it took the world by storm when it was first published.

The principle behind food combining is that different foods require different digestive enzymes. Eating too many different types of food at one meal will result in laborious digestion, whereas a properly combined meal will be easily digested, any associated digestive problems will be prevented and the food will be efficiently absorbed. The basics of proper food combining are as follows:

- eat nothing but fruit until 12 o'clock noon
- eat fruit on its own, never with any other food, as it is very easily digested (within approximately half an hour); fruit supplies nutrients almost instantly and eating it with other foods just prolongs the digestion and absorption, and can also cause fermentation when it is partly digested and mixed with other food; fermentation leads to excess gas and bloatedness
- proteins and vegetables (including salad) can be eaten together
- starches and vegetables (including salad) can be eaten together
- proteins and starches cannot be eaten together

Can herbs make me feel hyperactive or nervous?

The appetite suppressants and most of the slimming mixtures available from your pharmacy contain a central nervous system stimulant. Unlike them, the herbal formula for slimmers cannot overstimulate your body.

There are two broad categories of drugs (appetite suppressants and bulking agents) available from your pharmacy for the treatment of excess fat, but even these have to be taken while on a kilojoule controlled diet.

Central nervous system stimulants have a boosting effect on the central nervous system. Their action depends on their ability to suppress appetite via messages sent along nerve pathways to the appetite controlling gland in the brain. These appetite suppressants can only be used for short periods of time because the body builds up a tolerance, and ever increasing dosages would be required for the desired effect.

In the second category, bulking agents create a sensation of fullness in the stomach. The drug is taken with water before meals and swells in the stomach. The theory is that if an overweight person feels full, they won't be overcome by the feeling of emptiness and lack of fulfilment which may cause failure to lose weight. The bulking agents have no effect on the central nervous system, so they won't cause irritability and nervousness. However, prolonged use of these agents can lead to constipation and the enlargement of the stomach capacity, which will result in increased hunger pangs when the agents are no longer in use.

The herbal formula does not have a stimulating effect on the central nervous system so there are no side effects in this regard. However, during the first ten days of taking the formula, a range of regulatory symptoms may appear, the severity of which depends on your present state of health. If you have been abusing your body with cigarettes, alcohol, coffee and poor eating habits, you might feel dizzy and nauseous.

The reason for this is different from the reason that causes dizziness and nausea when taking appetite suppressants. Both are symptoms of high levels of poisons in the bloodstream, but while taking herbs the toxins are on their way out of the body, when taking appetite suppressants they are on their way in.

When the symptoms pass while taking herbs, you know that your body has been cleansed and regulated and is now working much better, whereas after taking appetite suppressants you feel dreadful, with low energy, bad moods and a general feeling of malaise.

Should I drink a lot of water while taking herbs?

The only time you need to increase your fluid intake is during periods of intense detoxification, and you will know that you need to increase your fluid intake because your urine will become very strong, darkly coloured and might have a stronger smell than usual.

Otherwise drink only when you are thirsty, but make sure it is something thirst quenching, not one of the mixtures of flavours and chemicals popular more for their taste than due to real thirst. If you are thirsty, try to drink water as much as possible. Eating a diet rich in foods with a high water content will supply your body with good quality fluid.

The recent fashion of drinking as much water as possible, supposedly in order to flush the toxins out of the body, does not at all increase the release of toxins from the cells in any way and puts an unnecessary strain on the kidneys. An increased water intake serves merely to dilute the toxins carried along in the bloodstream, so that there are no high concentrations which could produce uncomfortable symptoms.

Can I drink alcohol while taking herbs?

"I have been taking your herbs for slimmers for one month and found that my eating patterns changed, because I used to eat late at night. I only lost 2.5 kg (5 lb). But I decided not to give up and when I had finished my second bottle, I had lost 7 kg (15 lb). My headaches decreased and I still enjoy my glass of wine every night. Is there no pharmacy in Bothaville that stocks your herbs for slimmers because to order by mail order takes too long."   Rena Angel, Bothaville

Alcohol, in moderation, can actually be good for you. The latest finds revealed that a glass of red wine with your meals can help to lower the incidence of cardiovascular disease. This has resulted in a scramble among scientists trying to determine exactly which substance in the red wine is responsible for the protective factor, so that it can be isolated and marketed in pill form. However, it is far more pleasurable instead, to enjoy a good glass of red wine with your meal.

Beer, particularly the milk stout variety, is rich in vitamin B complex and a very good drink to have in the evening if you suffer from insomnia, because hops is a natural sedative that will gently help to put you to sleep. Again, remember that one beer will suffice. I would suggest that you rather steer away from hard liquor such as brandy, whiskey and vodka, among others, as these contain precious little nutritive value and are a bit like sugar – they supply empty calories and, in order for the body to process the alcohol, valuable vitamins have to be leached from your system. Do not drink liqueurs at all. These are very rich in sugar and are of absolutely no nutritive benefit to your body.

Will taking herbs help me to lose weight if my weight problem is genetically based?

"I would just like to tell you that I have lost 4.5 kg (10 lb) in one month. Our family has a history of weight problems. After being warned by my doctor to lose weight because of my high blood pressure, I must admit I'm feeling great now and don't regret using Natruslim. I haven't picked up one ounce yet."   Mrs Hendricks, Matroosfontein

It is a fact that fat parents will very often produce fat children and it is thought that this phenomenon is due to the genetic inheritance of a certain 'fat gene'. However, this issue is still much debated today – scientists call it the nature versus nurture debate. The question is whether the children of overweight parents are themselves overweight because their parents are teaching them their own bad lifestyle habits, or whether these children put on excess weight simply because they have inherited the genetic predisposition to do so.

I think there are a number of ways to view the phenomenon of fat families. Firstly, I do believe that the habits of parents are primarily to blame. If the child begins to eat a bad diet and irregular meals from an early age, this will predispose the child to put on weight. Once weight is gained in childhood it is very difficult to shed later on in life.

The second factor is that often a certain organ weakness is passed on from the mother, or father, to the child. This may be a genetic defect, but since that concept always stirs horror in people because it implies an incurable condition, I would prefer to say that it is a weakness in the constitution, inherited from one or a combination of both the parents. This weakness need never develop into an acute illness, it is merely a susceptibility that requires certain factors to aggravate it. Therefore, if a child has inherited the susceptibility to becoming fat, it will only start gaining weight if aggravating factors, such as irregular meals, poor diet, overeating, or an illness that strains the weak organ, exist. If, however, it was well looked after, ate a regular, healthy, balanced diet and didn't fall ill, this child could remain thin within the fat family.

There are three periods in a person's life where the body naturally creates new fat cells rather than growing and filling the existing ones:

- during the last few days before birth
- during the first two years of babyhood
- during the two years before puberty

Can I use herbs while I'm ill or should I wait until I'm well again before starting?

"I wish to congratulate you on your product. At last an item that does what it says. I developed cramps, a severe cough, and problems when urinating. Believe me, after using Natruslim as indicated for two days I felt relieved. It certainly does its job. In conclusion, as a pensioner, be assured I will remain a customer of your fine product." Leon Schwartz, Villiers

There is no need to wait until you can begin using the herbs. Sometimes people delay starting the formula because they first want to finish a course of medication, are waiting for a good time to start dieting (maybe until the festive season is over), or they are waiting until they start feeling better after an illness. Do not delay.

Once you have obtained the herbs, even if it happens to be the middle of the day, start taking them immediately. If you want to go on a diet, then starting the herbs will motivate you. If you are feeling unwell, the herbs will improve your health much quicker than if you were not taking them because they help your body to deal efficiently with any condition it may be suffering from.

Don't even wait to finish reading this book before you start taking the herbs. You can already start the herbal formula for slimmers, and then read the book while losing weight at the same time.

Can men use herbs for slimmers?

"My husband lost 10 kg (22 lb) with one bottle. It changed his life. He sleeps well, is calm and peaceful and a pleasure to the whole family." Eva Schimmig, Windhoek

I have written this book mainly for all the overweight women out there who are desperately struggling to lose weight, simply because the majority of slimmers are female. However, this is not to say that the formula is not effective for men too. In fact, men tend to lose weight a lot quicker and easier than most women.

Men's and women's bodies are structurally totally different, primarily because women are designed to bear children. They therefore have to be able to store enough nutrients within their bodies to enable a child to grow. Men do not have to have this facility, so their bodies do not naturally store much fat. If we compare a fit man with a fit woman, the woman will have at least 20 percent body fat, as opposed to 15 percent in a fit man.

A girl needs a certain amount of fat in order to develop into a woman and start menstruating. This is the body's insurance that she will have enough fat to nourish a baby one day. If a woman's fat levels drop below the healthy norm she may stop menstruating, as frequently happens with females suffering from anorexia.

The female hormone oestrogen encourages the body to lay down fat deposits in what a lot of women consider to be their problem areas: the hips, buttocks, thighs and breasts. Oestrogen is also responsible for women retaining fluid before their periods. The male hormone, on the other hand, promotes muscle growth, which means that a man's natural tendency is to lose weight and build muscle, thereby increasing his basal metabolic rate, resulting in more fat being burned up.

Pregnancy, of necessity, leads to increased fat deposits. Levels of the hormone progesterone rise during pregnancy and part of the response to this hormone is an increased appetite. Frequently women cannot lose weight after having gained some during pregnancy because they have grown more fat cells. So, no matter how much weight they lose, they will always weigh slightly more after having given birth than they did before.

What do you think of fasting?

For those of my readers who want to embark on a real health booster, fasting is an excellent way to focus on yourself and on your body. It requires discipline, strength and dedication to maintain a fast, which sometimes may be a good exercise to make you feel more in control of yourself.

Not only is fasting rewarding, both mentally and emotionally, it is also a good way to speed up the detoxification process. If you are in relatively good health then fasting for a short period of time (two weeks) is perfectly safe.

During a fast, the body starts breaking down protein and energy reserves stored in the healthy, as well as the diseased or unhealthy body tissues. This means that diseased tissue is digested and excreted. Hence, fasting is a useful treatment for tumours and inflammations, as well as excess fat tissue. When the stores run out and there are no more reserves left in the body, true hunger will return. The tongue will clear to a healthy pink colour, the secretion of saliva will be stimulated, the eyes will clear and the skin will look much healthier than before.

The faster will experience hunger during the first three days and then it will disappear. Juice-fasting is preferable to water-fasting, as it does supply some nutrients, which makes it a little easier to stick to the regimen. If you are using juices, make sure that they are freshly squeezed and do not contain any additives. Dilute them with some spring water, and drink the juice as though it were a meal, from three to five times daily, no more.

It is important to start and end a fast correctly. Start with one day of fruit, vegetables and salads only, followed by one day of fruit. The fast can start on the third day after this. Only fruit must be eaten on the first day of breaking the fast. Cooked vegetables may be introduced on the second day, and some grilled chicken or fish on the third.

Try not to get back into the bad habits you had before, like eating too much. Your stomach has now shrunk and won't need as much food as before to satisfy your hunger. If you keep eating small meals when you get hungry, you should be able to maintain a smaller stomach, which will also keep your appetite reduced.

While you are fasting, it is useful to do some focused thinking. Try and spend some time completely by yourself for at least half an hour a day. Enjoy a solitary walk among some greenery. Take a step back from yourself and have a good look at your life as a whole. Are you happy? If not, what are the reasons for your discontent? Think of a solution to your difficulties and try, as much as possible, to create the life you would truly enjoy living.

Have you always wanted to learn photography or get your pilot's license? Do you yearn to travel to faraway places? Think of the ways you can fulfil your dreams. Remember what you wanted to be when you were 16 years old? What happened to that dream? Are you now where you saw yourself then, and if not, are you happy with your present lifestyle?

Fasting is a great time for purifying your system, so make the most of it by clearing your mental and emotional cobwebs too. You'll be amazed at the feelings illicited by a period of abstinence.

Will menopausal women who are on HRT (hormone replacement therapy) lose weight using herbs?

"I used Natruslim for a few months but didn't lose weight. I am on HRT and find it extremely difficult to lose weight. I also retain a lot of fluid, sometimes my feet are so swollen my shoes do not fit well. I started losing weight when I used chaste tree together with the basic slimming formula. Not only am I now slowly losing weight but my water retention problem is much improved."　　　　　　　　　　　　　　　　　　　　　Aluana Swainston, Rivonia

Female sex hormones can be synthesised by the liver and from fat cells, so a cessation of the menses does not mean that absolutely no oestrogen is made by the body anymore. Therefore, it is not essential to take oral hormones unless organs like the liver, thyroid and adrenal glands are not working as they should.

Herbs are incredibly useful for women going through menopause. Not only will they help to maintain a healthy weight, they will also help to combat the uncomfortable symptoms often experienced during menopause. If you are experiencing a difficult menopause, and before you consider taking HRT, try taking 15 drops of chaste tree three times daily for at least a month. This herb regulates the activity of the female sex hormones, which means that it will balance your hormones and remove any of the associated symptoms.

If you are on HRT, take the herbs together with your medication. After a few months on the formula, when you start feeling in good shape, stop the HRT. Continue with the herbs and see how you fare. You can always start the HRT again should the unpleasant symptoms return.

In *Every Woman's Book*, Dr Paavo Airola offers an interesting perspective on HRT: "Now, most women confronted with the first distressing symptoms of menopause, such as hot flushes, run to their doctor, and the average doctor will immediately put them on oestrogen therapy. If he is a conventional doctor, he will most likely prescribe a diethylstilbestrol-type synthetic oestrogen. If the doctor is of the 'new breed' and nature-oriented, he may prescribe a more 'natural' form of oestrogen, a so-called conjugated hormone naturally occurring in pregnant mare (horse) urine, usually premarin. In whatever form, oestrogen therapy is not only completely unnecessary, but is a very dangerous way of trying to interfere with a natural process in this period of a woman's life."

HRT is aggressively marketed as a woman's wonder drug, stopping hot flushes, vaginal dryness, heart disease and cancer. It was also claimed to reverse the ageing process, increase libido and stop osteoporosis.

Now that HRT has been on the market for over 40 years it has been found effective only against the hot flushes and vaginal dryness, both of which are due to low oestrogen levels and, over time, the dangers of long-term use, similar to those found with the contraceptive pill, became apparent.

As with the contraceptive pill, there are certain high-risk individuals who should not take any hormone replacement therapy. These are women who smoke, and those with a history of breast disease, cancer, blood clots, arteriosclerosis, heart, liver or kidney disease.

Will the formula help against osteoporosis?

Many women use HRT as a means of protection against osteoporosis. The hormones are supposed to prevent calcium from being leached from the bones. However, the cause of osteoporosis is not just a lack of calcium in the diet, it is due to a faulty calcium metabolism, which is very closely linked to the thyroid and parathyroid glands. And, as you have read in this book, our thyroid glands suffer much abuse from today's lifestyles.

This means that our calcium metabolism can quite easily become disordered by the various stresses placed on the sensitive thyroid gland. Increasing your intake of calcium will not improve the situation and can even exacerbate the leaching of calcium from the bones.

The herbal formula for slimmers is an excellent prevention against osteoporosis, especially if it is combined with chaste tree. The herbs, together with a diet rich in seeds, yoghurt and dark green vegetables will insure you against developing osteoporosis as you age.

Care should be taken not to overdo it and take too many calcium supplements as they can also have an adverse effect, resulting in too much calcium in the body. Excessive amounts of calcium cannot be metabolised, which can result in the formation of kidney stones.

How much weight can I expect to lose?

The herbs work differently for everyone and therefore the rate of weight loss varies from person to person. However, I have found that, on average, people lose from 4–5 kg (9–11 lb) a month, that is if you have about 12 kg (26 lb) to lose.

When can I expect to start seeing results?

You'll begin to notice weight loss within a week to ten days. If you are not losing weight on the scales, you are almost definitely losing inches, so do not get disheartened. It might be a good idea to take body measurements before embarking on your weight-loss programme. In this way you will be able to record the reduction in your body size.

AFTERWORD

Obesity, besides the vanity aspect, poses a serious threat to our health and needs to be cured. I hope you put to use what you have learnt in this book. If you do, you are on your way to permanent weight loss. I have battled all my life to control my weight, reading book after book and trying many diets. Herbs are the easiest and safest solution to everybody's weight problem, no matter what the cause. Not only are they beneficial in regulating your weight, but, more importantly, they rectify your health at the same time. It is a very gratifying feeling to know that you are looking great both inside and out. You would not have lost weight successfully unless all your organs and internal systems were toned and working well. You are now insured against future ill health, both because you are much slimmer and also because you are in good health.

I recently had an experience that made me realise just how important it is to look after my own health and avoid the need for medical care. A hospital stay, for me, is a little like entering a chamber of horrors. All the machines, tubes and gleaming tools they have to treat us, remind me more of the torture dungeons of old than of a modern medical facility. The compassionate hands of the nursing sisters have, all too frequently, been replaced with humming apparatus. To avoid having to succumb to this treatment it is important to look after your health while you still have it.

Strengthen your body with herbs and you can prevent any inherited or stress-related weakness from developing into a full-blown disease or disorder. Not only will this save you money, it may prevent the trauma of serious medical intervention and perhaps save your own life, or that of someone dear to you.

AFTERWORD

The next step is up to you. I hope you will take it. Get on the programme today and get ready for a wondrous life change. Please let me know how you progress. If there is any way in which I can improve this book please let me know – we all benefit from sharing our stories and experiences.

Good luck,

GLOSSARY

Alterative
(used to be known as blood cleansers)
- restores the proper function of the body
- increases general health and vitality

Analgesic
- reduces pain

Anthelmintic
- destroys and gets rid of worms

Antibilious
- removes excess bile
- useful in biliary and jaundiced conditions

Anticatarrhal
- removes excess mucus from the body

Anti-emetic
- reduces nausea
- relieves vomiting

Anti-inflammatory
- soothes inflammations

Antilithic
- prevents and removes stones in the urinary system (kidney stones)

Antimicrobial
- helps the body to resist against and destroy harmful micro-organisms

Antispasmodic
- prevents and eases spasms and cramps

Aperient
- mild laxative

Aromatic
- strong aromas that are capable of stimulating the digestive system

Astringent
- reduces secretions and discharges
- contracts tissues

Bitter
- stimulates the digestive system

Cardiac tonic
- beneficial to the heart

Carminative
- stimulates the natural movement of the digestive system; relaxes the stomach
- helps against digestive gas; reduces colic

Cholagogue
- stimulates release of bile from the gall bladder
- has a laxative effect as bile is the body's internally produced laxative

Demulcent
- rich in mucilage (gelatinous fibre)
- soothes and protects inflamed internal tissue

Diaphoretic
- promotes perspiration which increases the elimination of toxins through the pores in the skin

Diuretic
- increases production and elimination of urine

Emetic
- causes vomiting

Emmenagogue
- stimulates and normalises menstrual flow

Expectorant
- helps in the removal of excess mucus from the respiratory system

Febrifuge
- helps to bring down fevers

Galactogogue
- increases the flow of the milk in breast-feeding mothers

Hepatic
- tones and strengthens the liver

Hypnotic
- induces a healthy, natural sleep

Mucilage
- contains a beneficial gelatinous fibre which soothes the mucous membranes

Nervine
- tones and strengthens the nervous system

Oxytocic
- stimulates the contraction of the uterus
- helps ensure an easy delivery in childbirth

Pectoral
- heals and strengthens the respiratory system

Rubefacient
- acts as a local irritant; stimulates the dilation of capillaries in the area, which increases the blood circulation and hastens the removal of impurities and relieves pain

Sedative
- reduces stress and nervousness
- calms the nerves

Sialagogue
- stimulates the secretion of saliva

Stimulant
- quickens physiological function of the body, resulting in increased energy

Tonic
- strengthens and enlivens the entire body and the targeted organs
- improves general health

Vulnerary
- applied externally to help heal wounds

ORDER FORM

✳   • Fax orders   (021) 461-1363

☎   • Telephone orders   (021) 462-1721 (have your credit card ready)

✉   • Postal orders   **Natruhealth CC**, PO Box 1971,

                            Cape Town, 8000, South Africa

        • Online orders   afrik@cis.co.za

Please send me .... copies of GET SLIM – STAY SLIM – NATURALLY by Dr Francesca Swainston.

I understand that I may return the book for a full refund if I am not fully satisfied, no questions asked.

Name: ....

Address: ....

....

....

Telephone   (code): .... (number): .... (home)

                 (code): .... (number): .... (work)

Shipping: Airmail R10 for the first book and R2 for each additional copy

Foreign orders: R30 extra

I enclose **R69.95** per book.   **Total: R**................................

Payment (please tick where applicable):

Cheque ☐   **Postal Orders** ☐   **VISA** ☐   **Mastercard** ☐

(cheques must be made payable to **Natruhealth CC**)

Card number: .... Exp. date:............ / ....

Name on card: ....

Signature: ....

ORDER FORM

✳	• Fax orders	(021) 461-1363
☎	• Telephone orders	(021) 462-1721 (have your credit card ready)
✉	• Postal orders	**Natruhealth CC**, PO Box 1971,
		Cape Town, 8000, South Africa
	• Online orders	afrik@cis.co.za

Herb 50 ml (2 fl oz) bottles	Qty	Unit price	Total
Natruslim® (basic formula)	....	R97.20	....
Bladderwrack	....	R32.50	....
Centaury	....	R35.75	....
Cleavers	....	R35.75	....
Chaste tree	....	R32.50	....
Dandelion	....	R31.20	....
Echinacea	....	R42.50	....
Hawthorn berries	....	R35.75	....
Liquorice	....	R46.95	....
Oats	....	R35.75	....
Shipping up to three bottles		R12.50	....
up to 10 bottles		R15.50	....
next day delivery	....	R20.00	....
Total		**R**	....

Name: ....

Address: ....

....

....

Telephone (code): .... (number): .... (home)

(code): .... (number): .... (work)

Payment (please tick where applicable):

Cheque ☐ **Postal Orders** ☐ **VISA** ☐ **Mastercard** ☐

(cheques must be made payable to **Natruhealth CC**)

Card number: .... Exp. date: ..../...........

Name on card: ....

Signature: ....

RECOMMENDED READING

- HOFFMANN, DAVID, *The New Whole Herbal*, Element Books.

- CALBOM, CHERIE and KEANE, MAUREEN, *Juicing for Life*, Avery Publishing.

- HAY, LOUISE, *You Can Heal Your Life*.

- CARPER, JEAN, *The Food Pharmacy*, Bantam Books.

- STEINMAN, DAVID, *Diet For A Poisoned Planet*, Ballantine Books.

INDEX

INDEX

INDEX

INDEX